The Suited Monk

Finding Your Life's Purpose and True Happiness

by

Raf Adams

The Suited Monk is a book for NOW. Raf's distinctive, easy-to-read narrative captures the essence of "the truth" contained in the ancient spiritual traditions in a way that's relevant for today. This is a must-read for all suited monks and nuns on "Life's Journey".
Matthew Chapple
Senior Vice President, Greater China, Mead Johnson Nutrition

At some stage of our lives, we inevitably reach certain crossroads—whether in our careers or personal lives—and this can present huge challenges and uncertainty. Raf's book gives clarity, guidance, and certainty when confronted with such challenges and is a must-read for anyone seeking direction, fulfilment, and enrichment during their life journey.
Jeremy Sargent
Chairman of the British Chamber of Commerce Guangdong

How to manage life is the challenge. Raf Adams demonstrates that happiness in life is attainable every day by understanding how we respond to the inner and external journeys. This is a book that can liberate the soul.
Professor Mike J. Thompson,
China Europe International Business School, Shanghai

Everyone who wants to enjoy life to the fullest should read *The Suited Monk.* Raf's Life Journey Model is a simple yet brilliant framework to help us understand why joy is not deduced from material wealth and why we should strive for inner peace and happiness. Reading *The Suited Monk*, I rapidly identified my own journey to bridge the gap between the inner and external world, which I will now accelerate to the fullest. Raf is a hero who will continue to affect positively the lives of his readers.
Peter Buytaert
Founder, Shanghai China Global Leaders (CGL) Management Consulting, Former President Asia at Agfa (Graphics)

Raf Adams's book *The Suited Monk* has been, and remains, one of the most useful tools helping me to understand, locate, and orient myself in the various situations, challenges, and circumstances my family and I face. Raf and his work are a constant point of reference and source of guidance, insight, and inspiration in my life. I highly recommend anyone looking for a more meaningful and happy life read *The Suited Monk*.

Dr. Dounald Thomas
Professor of International Marketing/Management
Guangzhou, China

Original and honest, this book captures the Life Journey workshop perfectly and is highly recommended as separate reading or as complementary follow up to one of Raf's workshops. I found this book so helpful (Simple language and model, to a complex topic, easy to read, truly a knowledgeable book) that I have already recommended numerous to both read the book and participate the workshop.

Henrik Larsen
Chairman of the Danish Chamber of Commerce South China

The Suited Monk "speaks" to you. Written in an engaging, conversational style, the weighty matter of finding your life's purpose has been decoded and broken down into some simple, easy-to-practice steps. Raf's Life Journey Model has been drawn from his and his workshop participants' rich (and real) experiences, and this is what makes it powerful and convincing.

Riktta Prasad
HR Director, R&D, Greater China at Unilever

We live in times of great uncertainty, but Raf provides us with great possibilities through his Life Journey Model. This model helps you see where you are in your life and what is the best journey for you to take. Raf's model will challenge you and take you to a new place of self-awakening. Raf's ability to tell his story and to then use the model to build a greater life for himself is truly inspirational and will motivate readers to do the same. A great read.

Bronwyn Bowery-Ireland
Former CEO, International Coach Academy

We should thank Raf Adams for showing us this simple but powerful path to reconciling the conflicts of life and career fulfilment. His story and insights struck a deep chord with MBA students at CEIBS. I'm glad that others can now access these lessons by reading Raf's book.

Lydia J. Price
Associate Dean, MBA Director
China Europe International Business School

Disclaimer

Every attempt has been made to ensure the accuracy and reliability of the information in this book. Neither the authors nor the publisher can be held responsible for any disadvantages readers might experience from the perusal of this book.

© Raf Verheyen, 2013

First published in January 2012 by WOW! The foundation for Applied Inspiration, a company registered in London number 3910512

Revised edition January 2013

ISBN 978-0-9570553-5-3

WOW! Books
The Hub
34B York Way
London NI 9AB

Table of Contents

Acknowledgements
Foreword by Dr. Mike Thompson

ACKNOWLEDGEMENTS

This book would not exist without the feedback, support, and input from many great people:

My mentor, business partner, and friend Dr. Mike Thompson, who has been a great adviser and offered fresh insights on the manuscript.

Micah Thompson, who did tremendous work on the final editing and proofreading of each chapter.

Jude Berman, who provided helpful editorial guidance to improve the manuscript.

The participants in my public speaking seminars, workshops and executive coaching clients, from whom I have learned so much and who have been instrumental in bringing this book to fruition. It has been my greatest privilege to know and work with each of you.

I would like to give special recognition to Ray Martin and Jeff Tan, whose insights on the book have been of immense value. Truly, without you it would never have become what it is.

Finally, there aren't enough words to thank my friend Grace Park, who has been one of my greatest supports on the journey of self-realization and continuous improvement as a person, reflecting on everything and giving her feedback.

And most importantly to you, the reader, who is helping me reach out to a wider network, to deliver a message I know must go out into the world.

FOREWORD

by Dr. Mike Thompson, Professor of Management Practice
China Europe International Business School

> *I have often thought that the best way to define a man's
> character would be to seek out the particular mental or
> moral attitude in which, when it came upon him, he felt
> himself most deeply and intensively active and alive. At
> such moments, there is a voice inside which speaks and
> says, "This is the real me".*

William James, *The Letters of William James*, 1878 [1]

For as long as I can remember, I have perceived life as a journey
in which one navigates the challenges, the joys, and the vistas
of distinct and different stages. Inevitably, our individual life
stages are the result of choices. Choices are limited by the
nature of our talents, the degree to which we require financial
security and the expectations of significant others. But most
importantly the limitations lie deep within: by our own self-
perception and the way in which we assess and deploy our
talents and capabilities. Of course, there is much stumbling, but
the hope of life is that we learn, we mature, and ultimately we
enjoy the reward of 'flourishment': the flourishing of our whole
unique personality and talents. I know that flourishment is not
an official word, but it is the closest made-up adjective that
seems to convey the completeness enjoyed by a person who has
practiced the virtues of life. Such a person has found the joys of
the good life in family, in community relationships, and in his
or her role in the wider world. Flourishment is the blossoming
of who we really are: the authentic self. In flourishment, as a
state of being, we find meaning, purpose, and happiness in life.

But how do we reach the state of flourishment? Well, you have

---

1.William James, The Letters of William James (Boston: The Atlantic Monthly Press, 1920).

in your hand an unusual, easy-to-read, and yet profound book, *The Suited Monk*, with a strong and clear message that meaning, purpose, and happiness in life are attainable During the past three years, Raf Adams has experienced a way of living that has helped him navigate the vicissitudes of life, handle disappointments, and enjoy the rich insights of his "inner monk". The inner self is so frequently masked out by what Raf calls the *external world*—the world we look out upon, which according to Raf, has no power to offer us lasting happiness. Our ego tells us that that satisfaction can be realised through achieving possessions and status in the external world. But as Raf points out, attaining our wants gives way to a feeling of insufficiency when the ego realises it has not been fully satisfied by external possessions or achievement. "Why do so many of us strive for external success when it ultimately fails to give us the fulfilment we're seeking?" is one of many challenges Raf poses in *The Suited Monk*. It is with challenges and claims like this that the message of *The Suited Monk* gently assaults the intellect and the rational, materialistic mode of thinking and world view to which we have become so readily attuned.

The Suited Monk does require spiritual acquiescence to what Raf refers to as guidance and insight from the universe—an all-pervasive energy that connects to our inner self and that can offer us prompts and insights along life's way if we could but recognise them. Although Raf defines universe as a force that might be considered as a higher power, or God, he does not engage in a religious or philosophical discussion; rather, he accepts that an energy is available to help us to live a purposeful, meaningful, and happy life. So, for example, unforeseen events may be interpreted as messages from the universe to let us know that a change is needed. But our ego may fear change and therefore reject or not even hear the messages that are sent our way. Recognising the messages, observing one's environment, and attuning oneself to what might be emerging for us, and then making choices and decisions is an exciting, yet risky, way of life.

When Raf first told me his story and the discovery he made about following his heart (inner self) and developing his inner world, not simply conforming to the external world, it helped me make sense of the distinctive intuitions and perceptions I also had experienced. I remember, for example, that during a flight from Shanghai to London in October 2008, I experienced a powerful inner sense, a vision (perhaps a call) that I should move to Shanghai. Yet no one had invited me! Although I was surprised by the strong sense that this was a next life step for me, I did not feel frightened by the prospect. Shanghai was not in my mind or plan at all, but I chose not to close down the impression I had received, but rather to explore it, discuss it with family and friends, and weigh it. The Shanghai plan emerged as I kept my inner eyes open to the events and the opportunities that opened up for me over the following four months before we made the final decision to move. I had known and responded to such intuitions before, and in each case, there were plenty of rational reasons not to respond to them—mainly the risk of getting it wrong and facing the loss of security (and maybe status) of my circumstances at the time.

Perhaps you, too, have experienced such intuitions. *The Suited Monk* will help you make sense of those occasions when you have really acted in line with your inner self, rather than following the requirements pushed upon you from the external world. *The Suited Monk* has the possibility of increasing our sensitivity to the signs and prompts from what Raf refers to as the universe. Seeing the unseeable requires faith, which is a modus operandi we use in circumstances in which we have no certainties or rational explanations to go on. This kind of faith may point us toward the possibility of a divine and loving being, although Raf is careful not to tread any particular religious path. However, as neuroscientific and psychological studies in the field of consciousness and self-identity demonstrate, these dimensions of human experience are easier to observe and describe than to explain. Faith is a non-rational and highly personal explanation that lies beyond the realm of scientific inquiry. Faith touches the heart and tantalises the intellect.

Raf writes honestly about his own early life of unhappiness and sense of failure, and about maintaining a respectable professional career while inwardly feeling empty and deeply unhappy. But as Raf began to listen to the voice within and took charge of his destiny, his life radically changed. How his life was transformed is the story of *The Suited Monk*. Raf is a remarkable and unusual man. His vision and insight are clear, and I believe his motive is to help people in their journeys of life. It has been my privilege to journey along with Raf after first meeting him nearly three years ago, and to understand something of his heart toward people and the world. A message as strong and as clear as the one Raf delivers may result in accusations of arrogance, but I believe Raf is essentially a humble man with a passion to share his experiences and insights widely. I have enjoyed sharing a little of his own journey and witnessing the genuine joy and happiness that shines through from his own life and work. I have seen business people and MBA students touched and engaged by Raf's message and he now has a company of people joined in what is becoming a shared mission through which we firstly truly discover ourselves and then learn to live peaceably and with grace amongst the people who surround our lives.

Although the message of living in flourishment has been present within streams of thought over the ages, the message of *The Suited Monk* comes with the freshness of one man's version based on his own experiences and marvellous insights. Raf Adams has found a way of life in which he finds himself happy every day in his soul, despite the physical and material pressures of everyday urban life – and I am a witness. This book is his answer to the historical quest of humanity to change for the better—to find peace; to live more harmoniously; to change the way society works with respect to business, education, health care, the challenges faced by developing world, the preservation of planetary resources, and its governance. We all know that the most interesting changes emerge from within as we begin to recognise who we could become and how much more we may achieve and give into the world.

As Leo Tolstoy wrote,

> There can be only one permanent revolution—a moral one; the regeneration of the inner man. How is this revolution to take place? Nobody knows how it will take place in humanity, but every man feels it clearly in himself. And yet in our world everybody thinks of changing humanity, and nobody thinks of changing himself.[2]

If you want to think about changing yourself and your life journey, read on...

Mike Thompson

Shanghai
January, 2013

---

2. Leo Tolstoy, "Three Methods of Reform" in Pamphlets, translated from the Russian (1900) as translated by Aylmer Maude in Redfern, P., Tolstoy: A Study, (London: A.C. Fifield, 1907), p. 100.

Chapter 1

In Search Of Meaning, Purpose And Happiness

1. In Search of Meaning, Purpose and Happiness

Once, a monk lived in a cave high on a mountain. He sought solitude because he wanted to experience peace and happiness. Each day he spent hours in blissful meditation, communing with nature. This, he told himself, was the purpose of human existence! He had found what he was looking for.

Then one day it occurred to him others should benefit from what he had realised. So with a smile in his heart, he came down from the mountain. As he stepped into the crowded marketplace, a man jostled him. As the monk moved aside, a bicycle speeding by narrowly missed him. He shook his head and thought; these people need some peace in their lives. It was good he had arrived.

Just then a woman dropped her heavy basket. The monk wasn't looking and before he knew it, he was skidding on squashed tomatoes. Without thinking, he grabbed for the woman's arm. "You!" he cried, a snarl on his face. "Watch out! Who do you think I am?!"

I like this story because though we may not be monks, many of us are like this. We don't see how easily we lose whatever happiness we have managed to gain. One little thing goes wrong, and the smile is wiped off our face. Like this monk, we suffer from a huge gap between our inner world and our outer reality, and the worst thing about it is that we don't even realise this is our predicament. Nor do we realise that true, unshakable happiness, the kind that will give lasting meaning to our life, is possible.

Growing up, I wasn't particularly happy. My relationships weren't filled with love and when I got older, rather than being a source of enjoyment, my job put me under constant stress and pressure to achieve. I found it difficult to relate to people, and although I tried to make myself fit into the world around me, that strategy never seemed to work. For twenty-seven years I struggled with feelings of inadequacy, depression, and self doubt the full gamut of negative emotions. Bottom line, you could say I was pretty miserable.

Then, a few years ago, everything changed. What previously was darkness became light. Within three years I was fortunate enough to find love and a renewed meaning and purpose in life. Now every single day, even in the most adverse conditions, I feel at peace within myself. Everything I experience within myself feels perfect exactly the way it is, and I enjoy the journey of my life to its fullest. In the next chapters, I will explain more about how this transformation came about. But for the moment, let me just say it was a radical shift, and made my life as it is today a truly fulfilling experience—from the moment I wake up until the moment I go to sleep, both in my work and my relationships. Sure, I still make mistakes in relating to people—I'm not perfect—but I have no anxiety or negativity because I am free from the ways of thinking that used to limit my potential for being totally fulfilled.

Here's the greatest miracle. I am not sitting by myself in a cave somewhere. I am an entrepreneur who wears a business suit and enjoys his work every day in the business world, yet at the same time I feel spiritually rich. I have come to think of myself as a suited monk. That is, I have found the inner peace, life purpose, and happiness one assumes might come only from living a dedicated spiritual life, locked away in a cloister or on a mountain top, and yet I enjoy all the material things the world has to offer. In other words, I live an integrated life.

Find Happiness in Your Life as It Is Right Now

The transformation that happened to me is not uniquely mine. Nor is it something that should be turned into classified information. It's something that belongs to all of us; it's our birthright as human beings. We all have a right to grow as individuals and find true happiness. In my work as a coach, public speaker, and workshop leader, I am constantly reminded that most people are seeking something more in their lives They want more happiness, more joy, and more purpose or meaning in their work and relationships. Many people struggle in today's environment to sustain happiness in such a fast-paced world. Everyone wants to be connected with his or her own self, to love and be loved, yet so few know how to create a truly satisfied and fulfilling life for themselves. This is not because they don't care, but because they don't know where to find the answers they seek.

In this book I explain how you, too, can find happiness and learn to let go of negativity and fear. I share not only stories from my own journey, but also from participants who took my workshops and coaching clients. Some of their names have been altered to respect their privacy.

Recently I met a forty-five-year-old businessman who was referred to me by one of my previous workshop participants. This man was successful in business, good looking, engaging and smart. But as he started to tell me about his situation, I could see tears forming in his eyes. I sensed a desperate sadness underlying his strong outer appearance. Even though his life was going well, with a stable job, good salary, nice house, and lovely wife and two kids, by all accounts he was on the verge of burnout. He sounded as though he was about to crack; about to lose it all. Why? His case is not unique. I see an epidemic of people all around facing the same challenges. I was one of those people myself a few years ago. Yet, with the right guidance, I believe everyone can find lasting happiness and purpose.

My invitation to you is to discover your own inner self—who you truly are. Find out what makes you happy and what gives meaning and purpose to your life. In other words, find your own inner monk.

This book does not adhere to or reflect any particular religious organisation or path. When I say "monk", I am not referring to any religious tradition, belief system or culture. Rather, I use it as a metaphor to capture the essence of the true self that transcends all religions and faiths. Unfortunately, no single word clearly conveys the meaning of this truth. Some people like to call it a higher power or God. In this book, I have chosen to refer to it as either the *true self* or *inner self*.

The more we experience our inner monk, the more we see that its power is not different from the power that runs the entire universe. For this reason, I also refer to this energy at times as the *universe*.

Experiencing the inner self is about getting in touch with a deep well of strength within. A suited monk is comfortable in his business suit (or her business outfit, as the case may be), knowing that unlike the power of the inner self, this external costume is as changeable as any fad or fashion. One of my clients, a fifty-two-year-old French man, recently shared that his wife left him after twenty-five years of marriage. He said, "Of all the people in the world, I wouldn't expect this would happen to *me*". For some reason, he thought he was immune to the winds of change. But when happiness is dependent on other people, your job, or places and events, it can disappear in the blink of an eye.

Our minds tend to focus so much attention on the external world, yet nothing in the external world has the power to give us lasting happiness. The only thing we can be completely certain about in the external world is change. We forget that all of a sudden an earthquake could wipe the slate clean, we could be fired from our job, our house could catch fire and all our possessions are lost, or our friends and loved ones could die or simply walk away from us.

When we believe that something on the outside is *making* us happy, we then depend on *having* this thing in order to feel happy. Our happiness is derived from our surroundings and as soon as something out there changes, we are affected by it—for better or for worse. We need to turn this around. Instead of habitually looking outside ourselves, we need to develop the awareness to look within and become more mindful. When you make the effort to do this, you will unlock the key to happiness. You'll be able to say, "I'm happy just the way I am. I'm completely fulfilled, no matter what happens around me". This internal state of being is not dependent on your surroundings and you can experience it anytime, anywhere. You can experience it right now in your life just as it is and in every moment thereafter.

All too often, we find ourselves going to battle in the external world, thinking that it is necessary in order to be successful. We think we need to take control of every situation to get what we really want. But even when we do seemingly conquer the world and achieve that glorious moment of pleasure—we get that sought-after promotion, the perfect wife or husband, the most prized piece of property—we find within a very short space of time we're back in search of the next thing. The thing that made us happy yesterday is merely a pale shadow of happiness today. "Great, I got it", we think with little or no pause, "now what else can I get?" More, more, more; bigger, better, greater, grander; more luxury, more glamour, more serenity, more perfection. But where does all this lead? We believe that if we achieve, gather, and retain all these things after a lifetime of clamouring for success, the points we've won will add up to and give us happiness. "All that's needed", we think, "is to work hard". So we put our dreams on hold until later, when we think we'll be in a better position to realise them.

How to Use This Book for Your Greatest Benefit

This book is designed to help you discover your own inner world; your true self; your own inner monk. The inner world is where you can find lasting happiness and purpose. Once you find that, you can manifest it in the external world of career, job, and responsibilities. Because we live in both worlds, they naturally develop in sync.

This book will guide and advise you on your life journey. The model I use is consistent with the collective wisdom of the world's greatest spiritual traditions and teachers. Whether you are working for a corporation as a CEO, or you are an accountant, policeman, lawyer or teacher, you can find happiness and purpose. The peaceful, complete and joyful state of being to which the insights in this book point is wholly yours. It is your right as a human being to experience these truths in your life. Each chapter conveys its own message and introduces you to another step on your internal journey. You also will learn how to integrate this internal journey with your day-to-day job. You will have and receive everything you need to live in the flow of life and to lead a comfortable and happy life and career.

After sharing the story of my own transformation (chapter 2), I explain the Life Journey Model, which is a visual representation of your life journey (chapter 3). I then talk about aspects of the external world and how we constantly search for satisfaction from other people and things, while at the same time, we feel disconnected because we identify primarily with the egoic mind, which is by nature prone to feeling unhappy and dissatisfied (chapter 4). If we want to become free of the *egoic mind* and find peace, it is helpful to first recognise what is *not* our true self, so we can discover what our true self is and how to cultivate that experience. The more we identify with our external world and external suit, the emptier we feel. We suffer and feel pain because we are increasingly disconnected from ourselves. This is what I call the *Gap* (chapter 5). The remaining chapters guide you through your own awakening and reconnection with your true self. You will learn about the laws of rejection and acceptance (chapter 6); learn how to bridge the Gap (chapter 7); discover your inner monk (chapter 8); and take a giant step toward finding true love, your inner self, and your life's purpose (chapters 9 and 10). Some chapters (especially 7 and 8) include practical exercises you can do to apply the principles in your life. You may find some exercises resonate better than others; please take what works for you and leave the rest.

Are you ready to experience a fulfilling life at work, in relationships, at home, and within yourself? Are you ready to start the journey of *The Suited Monk*?

Chapter 2

How The Journey Begins

2. How The Journey Begins

Ray, a friend of mine in England who was a businessman, told me that ten years ago he would have described himself as happily married, running a successful company, and living in a beautiful home in London. He had recently received the *Daily Telegraph's* Business Leader of the Year award. He enjoyed his affluent lifestyle and he and his wife were about to start a family. Everything in his life was apparently going very well.

Then—boom! Within a six-month period, his wife had a miscarriage, the couple separated, and eventually they divorced. Because his wife was also his business partner, this led to the destabilisation of his business, and eventually its demise. As if that weren't enough, his father died suddenly. Everything converged to create a very short and intense period of calamitous suffering.

It came as a complete shock, he told me. The experience was like watching a bomb drop on his life, and then afterwards standing in the massive crater that had been created and looking at all the debris and smoke, whilst feeling an overwhelming sense of devastation, fear, loss, and uncertainty about the future. That was his wake-up call, which ultimately led him to set a new and different direction for his life. He was forty-three-years-old when it happened.

The Wake-up Call

You can begin your life journey at a number of possible starting points, and the wake-up call you receive can be pleasant or unpleasant. For example, it can happen simply by reading an article, attending a workshop or talking to a friend. It can also manifest as burnout in your career, a divorce, an accident, drug addiction, the loss of a job, or betrayal by someone you love. It can appear in the form of an illness or a near-death experience. You may become aware that you are not on the right track or that you have been trying to be someone you are not. Any of these events or insights can create an opening that leads you to search for greater clarity, awareness, and purpose.

When you get this wake-up call and start to become more aware of yourself and your life condition, you begin to ask questions such as: "What am I here for?"; "What is my life all about?"; "I've been working very hard, why am I still looking a sense of true happiness?", and "What should I do with my life?"

My own journey started in 2006 at the age of twenty-seven. I was a high achiever working in a freight-forwarding company in South China, and was focused only on my corporate suit in life. Two years later, I was one of the best sales performers in the region, with a contract in my hand to become European sales director and report directly to the CEO of a shipping company with 5,000 employees. Then, suddenly I was fired. There I was, without a job, and no idea where to go or what to do next. That's when my journey started.

Wake-up calls are often necessary because it is through these experiences that our inner monk opens his eyes and awakens. You can think of your inner monk as your friend and guide for your life's journey. Your guide helps you make decisions and protects you so you can move forward on your journey. Know that you're not alone on this journey.

You actually already have this guide within you, but you probably haven't become aware of or created a relationship with your guide yet. Often people buy a computer with pre-installed software on it, but don't bother to use it. They never realise how it might benefit them. Our inner monk is like that. He is already installed in our body but we haven't made use of him. We haven't let him speak to us. So it's time to wake up your guide! It's a free service, so why not use it?

Some people tell me they do have a sense of inner guidance, but they don't necessarily trust it. In fact, I would say everyone has an inner monk that speaks to them from time to time. Their inner monk is awake for at least those few moments - that's a start. You just need to encourage your monk to wake up more fully. This will happen as you develop the ability to listen to and respond to his guidance.

As you make your way through life, you pay attention to the various roads and buildings you see around you in the real world. You listen to the radio and hear people talk. You do this even without thinking most of the time. In the same way that you pay attention to things in the external world, you want to give closer attention to what you feel, hear, and see within.

Often people are inclined to dismiss guidance they hear from within. It doesn't make sense to the logical mind, so they ignore it. We are not trained in school to value information or experiences that are alien to our minds. The mind is a comfort and security-driven machine, and it is designed to make protecting the status quo its priority. Thus, it will very likely dismiss information that comes its way if it thinks that information might fundamentally challenge its view of reality.

When your inner monk speaks up, your mind might initially overwrite his guidance. Sometimes you have to overwrite your own mind. That's the only way the unexplainable can be absorbed in your awareness. Initially, what your inner monk says might not have meaning to you. The true meaning will only come after a period of reflection. You have to build up this ability. It's a skill that improves over time. You learn gradually from experience which words of guidance you want to use and which are not meaningful to you.

Your Life Map

As we start the journey, most of us do not have our own tailor made map to guide us through life and help us make better decisions. By default, we have to follow directions using maps that are meant for others or for society in general. If you have your own map, however, you can make your own choices. You can choose your own life direction.

Have you ever felt you're being forced to fit into a mold you don't really fit into? Or that no one really recognises you for who you are? Or that you can't use your true talents in your job? Perhaps you have had thoughts like these. If so, you know what it feels like to navigate through life feeling lost and without a map. It can be a rather lonely feeling.

Remember Your Purpose

When your inner monk wakes up, he will remind you of many things you have forgotten. Early in life, as a child, you were naturally in touch with what you loved. You may have made promises to yourself, or told yourself about things you wanted to do in life. You had a sense of purpose for yourself. As you got older, much of this was forgotten during the daily course of life. But once your inner monk awakens and you're on the journey, don't be surprised if you suddenly remember what you had forgotten. All this is part of the unique map that is your life.

In my own case, aspects of my current life resonate with ideas and images that were present in my consciousness over the years. For example, a few years ago my mother reminded me that at the age of six I made the decision to become a priest. As a teenager, I started noticing Asian women on the streets of Belgium and had the feeling they would play a role in my future. At the age of twenty-four, I heard my boss give a presentation and I was struck by how knowledgeable, confident, and charismatic he was. He spoke with genuine authority and connected with the people in the room. I told myself that I wanted to be like that. So, if you put together these various fragments, it comes as no surprise that I currently live in Asia, I write books and conduct seminars about the life journey, and I regularly give public talks.

As Steve Jobs famously once said: "You can't connect the dots looking forward, you can only connect them looking backwards. So you have to trust that the dots will somehow connect in your future. You have to trust in something: your gut, destiny, life, karma, whatever. Because believing that the dots will connect down the road will give you the confidence to follow your heart, even when it leads you off the well-worn path".[3]

---

3. Steve Jobs, Commencement address, Stanford University, June 12, 2005.

At this moment, you may think your life has no truly satisfying purpose. But as your inner monk wakes up, you will find it easier to remember or recall or revisit ideas and inspirations you had, but later discounted or totally forgot.

Often, a purpose we set for ourselves goes by the wayside because we have built up certain beliefs based on the way we view the world and others. For example, we think, "I am too old for this", or "I am too young for that", or "I am not intelligent enough". If you have a corporate job, you may think you can't do anything that might rock the boat because you are thinking about your retirement, and that means steering clear of anything that could put your income at risk.

Many of the beliefs you hold may not be true, yet you cling to them anyway. You don't have a mechanism that allows you look at your beliefs from a distance and evaluate if they are true or not. As you start your journey, one of the first things your inner monk can do is provide you with that perspective. You see, your monk is the observer of your mind. So, instead of living in the limited world of your own beliefs, when your monk wakes up, you will learn to observe your mind. This book will help you to become an observer so you can make better life choices.

Clarify Your Purpose

In 2008, when I lost my job in South China, my partner suggested we go to Europe because she had always dreamed of living there. I found myself in a dilemma because I had no desire to return to Europe. My own purpose in life was becoming clear, and it was taking me in a different direction. Yet, I strongly considered my partner's suggestion because I wanted to make her happy. Fortunately, a job offer came up in Shanghai shortly thereafter and alleviated the situation completely. On the journey of life, events often take place that create dilemmas like this. It is a common feature of the journey, particularly at the start.

You may find yourself in a situation where at a deeper level you know that what you plan to do is not going to work out, but you can't see any better alternatives so you go with it, even though you suspect it won't turn out right. Ever had this kind of moment?

We may want to follow our dreams, but being true to ourselves is not always convenient. For example, perhaps you attended a social event simply because you thought, "I *should* do this", or you felt an obligation to someone else when you honestly would have preferred to do something completely different. I meet people who stay in jobs they don't feel good about because they think finding more satisfying work would require too much effort. These people settle for conditions that are not ideal for their development just because the status quo is more comfortable than stepping outside their comfort zone and taking a risk.

Feng, a participant in one of my workshops, had been married to a woman for fifteen years when it became clear to him the marriage should end. However, in preparation for divorce, his wife made a claim on his personal fortune. Feng panicked. To preserve his financial status, he decided to avoid divorce and instead arranged to live separately from his wife while still remaining legally married. He maintained this position for eight years, during which time he had no other relationships.

Feng's attachment to protecting his financial assets at all costs, and his reluctance to experience the emotions that would surface if he divorced his wife, caused him great suffering. It made it virtually impossible for him to open the door to finding true love. Eventually, after almost a decade, he realised that he couldn't defer his dreams any longer. He filed for divorce and paid the money requested by his wife. It was a lot of money, but he could afford it. Most importantly, he made a move to take ownership of his life. A couple of months later, Feng sent me an email saying he had started a new relationship and that he was much happier. He had resolved his long-term dilemma by letting go of the old, and immediately the new was ready to come in.

Another workshop participant, Joyce, got a job opportunity in Shanghai while she was working in Guangzhou. She weighed the benefits of taking the new job; a better salary, a better title in the company, and further enhancement in her career. She also weighed the benefits of keeping her current job; working with colleagues with whom she has great relationships, loving what she is doing already, and enjoying her life. It was clear both options could work for her.

It's not always obvious how we should act. Joyce had a dilemma because the pros and cons of the two jobs were evenly matched. They forced her to consider the subtle differences, rather than the most obvious differences. When she did this, deep down she knew if she took the job in Shanghai it would be a rational decision; one coming from her mind. As a result, she decided not to take the job.

However, after turning down the job offer, Joyce continued to wonder if she had made the right decision. It nagged at her. It was only when she discovered the Life Journey Model presented in this book that she was able to clarify that she had made the right choice. The model gave her a map she could use to understand her life. Using that map allowed her to fulfill her purpose with greater certainty.

Courageous people are able to walk in uncertainty because they have a mental map they use. If you know someone like that, you can check it out with them and they will tell you how they do it.

Life has its own flow. At any juncture, it can present circumstances that allow you to change the direction of your journey. Of course, this is not always clear in the moment. A situation can arise in which you don't immediately recognise what is best for your own growth. This is especially the case if the situation is something you don't like (such as an accident or getting fired), or if it something unexpected or not in line with your plans. However, even if you don't like it, it can be a very powerful gift for you and you shouldn't discard it.

Often we don't understand until later why things are happening as they are. For example, Steve Jobs took a class in calligraphy, even though at the time, it was not clear to him why he was doing so. Only when he realised six or seven years later that calligraphy was the key to creating new kinds of fonts for Apple computers, did he suddenly see why it was important for him to take that class.

With hindsight, you can see why you did something. But at the time you did it, it may not have made sense. Often there is a big time delay before you can clarify what is best or most meaningful for you. The important thing is to recognise that these events are opportunities.

Moreover, your inner monk is a junior player in the scenario. You get a message from what I like to call the CEO of Life—our ultimate boss. In the form of life's events and circumstances, he gives you direct instructions, which are beyond what you get from your inner monk. Then you clarify with your monk how to fulfill your purpose.

Live Your Purpose

Once you are on your path, the things you need will come to you quite easily. You might be wondering, "How do I know if I am on the right path?" When you live in the flow of life and notice that things are happening easily and for the right reason with limited effort on your part, you can know that you are on the right journey.

As you are walking on your true journey, life has wondrous gifts to give to you; things you cannot see, nor explain. For example, as I was on my journey toward becoming a public speaker, I woke up in my apartment one morning and suddenly received a state of total and all-encompassing bliss. It was so intense I couldn't do anything except walk to my couch and sit down. I could only *be* in that blissful state. I felt as though I existed outside the mundane world, in an internal realm that was unimaginably wonderful. I could sense a great energy surrounding me. I couldn't see it with my physical eyes but I could feel it. And with it came the feeling of wholeness; completeness. Nothing needed to be added and nothing could be taken away.

You could say it was like living my life for twenty-seven years as a single drop of water, and then suddenly that drop fell into and merged with the entire ocean. The drop had been capable of feeling moments of intense happiness, but nothing compared with the limitless bliss awash in the ocean.

There had been no indication beforehand that this would happen; I didn't search for this experience. And although it made perfect sense in the moment, my mind couldn't make sense of it afterward. From the limited research I had done up to that point, I didn't even know these kinds of experiences existed.

So I did more research to clarify what had happened to me. I investigated the ancient wisdom of the world's various religious and spiritual traditions. As I read books and listened to audiotapes about spirituality and the deeper meaning of life, it was clear that what I had experienced was a spiritual awakening, akin to what had been described in different ways by all these traditions.

The intensity of my experience did not last, and eventually I was able to resume my normal activities. But its essence has stayed with me. From that moment on, I have been in touch with my true self. You may be wondering, "Can I transform *my* life? Can my everyday life really be as perfect as I want it to be?" You may wonder if you also can have an awakening moment, find true love, and live in total happiness.

The answer is yes. I fully believe that what I, as well as others attending my workshops have experienced is equally possible for you. And why not? In all the ways that matter, you and I are not different. I don't know if exactly what happened to me will happen to you. Probably not. But that's not important. Everyone's journey in life is unique. You have to live *your* purpose, not my purpose. If you establish yourself on the right path and cultivate a strong relationship with your inner monk, your purpose in life will reveal itself to you.

Even if you have to make tough choices, things will work out just fine. In fact, the more you do it, the easier it becomes. This may sound like a cliché, but as the Buddha supposedly said, "No one saves us but ourselves. No one can and no one may. We ourselves must walk the path".

In this book, I share what you can do today to make your life more meaningful. I explain how you can take the first step on

35

your journey of life, and guide you through the process of turning unhappiness into happiness and negative emotions into positive emotions. I show you how to find your true purpose and give you an understanding about how the journey of life evolves.

Most of us have daily jobs and a family to take care of. It's neither possible, nor desirable, for many of us to meditate in a cave twenty-four hours a day, live in a monastery, sit in a temple for hours on end, or dedicate our everyday life to the pursuit of our spiritual development. However, there is a way to do the inner work you need to do while continuing to live your existing life. Therefore, this book is intended to bridge the gap between the external world you live in and your internal world; between your mind and your heart.

The search for deeper meaning in life is not only for spiritual seekers or teachers. It is for you and I, children and parents, business people, and everyone around us. Just as the Buddha and other spiritual masters followed their highest destiny, it is up to each of us to go through the journey of self-discovery that is available to us now. Because your destination is different from that of each other individual, I can't tell you specifically what your destination is. However, all our journeys have similar patterns, so we can learn from each other.

From the day you are born until the day you die, you live your life. Whether you are a CEO, an entrepreneur, a writer, a baker, a student or you are unemployed, you have a choice to make. You can move through life feeling lost and unfulfilled inside and basing your decisions about career and relationships on the safety and comfort you feel you need, or you can embark on your life as a conscious journey. The latter is the journey of self-realisation, of letting go of the old and gaining the new, of walking the path that is destined for you so you can feel fulfilled in your heart.

If you are willing to walk the journey that has been laid out for you, to establish a relationship with your inner monk, to find your purpose, and to learn from all the beautiful gifts life has to offer you, then you are ready to use the model presented to you in the next chapter.

Welcome to the journey!

Chapter 3

The Life Journey Model

3. The Life Journey Model

Imagine it's the weekend, you are sitting at home with your wife or husband and you are making plans to go on holiday. What is the first thing you need to know? Where you want to go, right? Maybe it's a city, or the mountains, or a special resort. Once you have the place picked out, what do you need to get you there? Obviously, you need a map.

Wouldn't it be nice if you had a map for life that could help you navigate and be clear about your direction in life, career, relationships, and spirituality? You would know you were on track. And if you ever got lost, you could turn to the map and easily find your way back onto the right path.

The Life Journey Model is such a map. It is a visual representation of the journey you take throughout your life, from birth to death. Its purpose is to offer fresh insight into age-old wisdom in a visual way, giving shape to humanity's common experiences on the journey of your life. It is presented here as a tool for you to use during your journey to help you navigate.

One man, a successful entrepreneur in his forties, told me that he found the model served as a "roadmap" for life; something he had searched for over many years. You can use the model to clarify your path to happiness in today's world, including how to overcome the various obstacles and challenges you may face. It can help you to bridge the gap you may feel between the spiritual world of your inner monk and the everyday reality of the suit you wear.

Origins of the Model

When I developed this model, I drew upon my own life experiences first. Afterwards, when I was reading books about the world's spiritual traditions, it became clear that the model reflected the wisdom found in these books. Incorporating that wisdom into the model made it even more powerful, because now people living in today's world can have the opportunity to grasp a complex understanding of life and spirituality in simple and easily understood terms. Later, I checked the model with people who attended my workshop, coaching clients, and others I interviewed who said they had found their purpose and lasting happiness. Very similar patterns emerged among all these individuals, and all were highly congruent with the model.

The world's religious and mystical traditions have led people on the journey of life since the beginning of time. In Christianity in one of the four gospels, John says that Jesus came so that "when He, the Spirit of truth, comes, He will guide you into all the truth; for He will not speak on His own initiative, but whatever He hears, He will speak; and He will disclose to you what is to come".[4] In this case, "He" is the inner monk and so in other words, they would have access to their inner monk, and thus would find lasting happiness.

Buddhism teaches that one can reduce or end suffering. The end of suffering is equated with enlightenment, which is described as a state of being beyond the duality of happiness and unhappiness. The Buddha spoke about letting go of desires and living a peaceful and happy life. In Taoism, the Chinese word *tao* means path or way. The Tao is not different from what I call the journey of life. It refers to the flow of the universe, which keeps everything balanced and ordered. As described in the *Tao Te Ching,* Taoists believe in following the Tao and living a simple life in balance with nature and the divine.

Even modern writers have explained the journey of life. For

---

4. John 16:13, King James Bible, New American Standard Version (1995).

example, Swiss psychiatrist Carl Jung revolutionised his field by introducing two main concepts: the collective unconscious, which suggests that we are not all separate individuals; and synchronicity, which suggests that we can't understand everything in life through the mind alone. According to Jung, when you are on your life journey, "your vision will become clear only when you look into your heart". He further counseled that those who look to the external world live life as if in a dream and only those who are able to look within will awaken.

Joseph Campbell, the American mythologist whose ideas relied heavily on the theories of Jung, wrote about the journey of the hero in *The Hero with a Thousand Faces*.[5] On this journey, the hero—who can be anyone among us—conquers challenges, meets his love, and finds his purpose.

Psychiatrist M. Scott Peck wrote *The Road Less Traveled*, which became a bestseller in the 1980s, to describe his vision of spiritual evolution. He famously said of the journey of life, that "greater awareness comes slowly, piece by piece…. The path of spiritual growth is a path of lifelong learning…. The experience of spiritual power is basically a joyful one".[6]

Novelist Paulo Coelho wrote in *The Alchemist* [7] about a boy who left his home and went to Egypt. There he conquered many challenges, listened to the universal teachings, found love, and returned home a rich man. This novel explains what religions teach, but does so through story and metaphor.

It is important to me that this model not be identified with any particular belief system, religious group, or culture. I designed it so

---

5. Joseph Campbell, The Hero with a Thousand Faces (New York: Pantheon, 1949).
6. M. Scott Peck, The Road Less Traveled: A New Psychology of Love, Traditional Values and Spiritual Growth (New York: Simon & Schuster, 1978), 285–286.
7. Paulo Coelho, The Alchemist: A Fable About Following Your Dream (New York: Harper San Francisco, 1995).

that it respects people from all beliefs and cultures. If you choose to work with it, know that you don't need to give up or modify any of these aspects of your personal background to get the full benefits it offers.

Overview of the Model

When you try to discover who you are—whether through time-honored religious scriptures or through contemporary works of fiction—you may find inspiration in the words of others. One important question is: "How can you apply that wisdom in your own life?"

How to apply such wisdom may not seem obvious because universal truths are mysterious in nature. They are spiritual or mystical and often they are formulated in ways that seem obscure or incomprehensible. We have busy jobs and families to take care of, but we don't have time to sort all these things out—or so we tend to feel.

The Life Journey Model shows you how to bridge the gap between your external world (which is everything contained within your current reality, and everything you see, hear, think, and believe about the world around you; in fact, everything that is important to support the ego) and your internal world (which is your spirit, your purpose in life, and your deepest desires; that is, everything that nourishes your heart). Each of these worlds is represented by an arc in the diagram (Figure 1). The arcs correspond to our progression through the various stages of childhood, adolescence, and adulthood.

If you look at the model and follow the arc of your external journey, you will see it moves in the direction of the ego; that is, toward the personality and sense of self you put forward to the external world. For this reason, I also refer to it as the "suit" you wear in the world. If you focus exclusively on the suit you are wearing you can have great success, but your inner world may still feel empty.

The arc of the internal journey, on the other hand, moves in the direction of the heart or who you are in your innermost being i.e. your inner self or inner monk. Focusing on your inner monk will invite awakening to the experience of deep and lasting peace and happiness. Of course, for that happiness to be truly lasting, the suit and the monk must be fully integrated. I'll talk more about that in the next chapter.

For now, to summarise, the ego/suit is characterised by the experience of separation from others, the world, and even your own self. The spirit/monk is characterised by the experience of oneness and the sense of being complete and whole within yourself.

Figure 1. The Life Journey Model

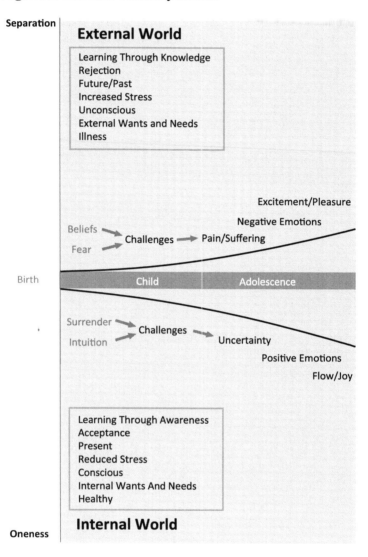

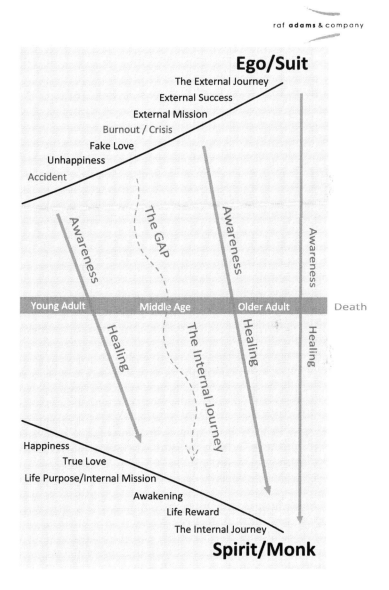

raf **adams** & company

Ego/Suit

The External Journey

External Success

External Mission

Burnout / Crisis

Fake Love

Unhappiness

Accident

The GAP

Awareness

Awareness

Awareness

Young Adult   Middle Age   Older Adult   Death

Healing

The Internal Journey

Healing

Healing

Healing

Happiness

True Love

Life Purpose/Internal Mission

Awakening

Life Reward

The Internal Journey

Spirit/Monk

Download a copy of the model at http://www.suitedmonk.com

External Versus Internal

The external and internal worlds are diametrically opposed. For example, everything in the external world is subject to change. Whatever you experience in the external world can be finished or ended, such as a job or a relationship. The core of your internal world, on the other hand, is eternal. When you experience something fully in your internal world, it will always be there for you. If you find true happiness within yourself, no one will be able to take it away from you. In fact, this is how you know whether you have found true happiness. If someone criticises you causing you to lose your feeling of happiness, then that feeling was part of your changing external world, but if the happiness remains no matter what anyone says or does, then you know it comes from the core of your internal world and it is eternal.

We deal with the external world primarily through our mind, beliefs, and fears, while constantly attempting to shield our ego. In the internal world, we learn to rely on intuition and surrender. By surrender I mean simply allowing things to happen as they are, without trying to force them to be the way you think they should be. In other words, going with the flow, rather than forcing your own agenda. When you surrender in this manner and don't limit yourself to what you already know, you open yourself to greater possibilities and more of them. It is through these unanticipated possibilities and the many unexpected opportunities that come your way, that you are able to discover and nurture your inner self.

You may think surrender has a negative connotation. For instance, you may equate surrender with giving up; feeling defeated; or worse yet, submitting to someone else's will. The kind of surrender I am talking about feels more like stepping outside your own objections and temporarily suspending your own judgement about why something may or may not work out.

Having faith is important when it comes to surrender. Faith means being willing to act even without evidence that what you are doing will turn out the way you want. On the life journey, one of the things you will learn is to have faith in, or trust what you discover in your internal world.

The external world brings us the experience of rejection, while the internal world generates acceptance. This is because the external world increases stress, while the internal world has the power to reduce it. We experience this all the time in small ways, though often we aren't aware of it.

For example, suppose something unpleasant happens at work. You naturally tense up from the stress and do your best to escape (i.e. reject) what is happening. Even if you feel you can't escape the actual situation, you can sit down for a few minutes and close your eyes and feel what's going on in your inner world. If during these moments you really allow yourself to feel and embrace what's going on without trying to change it, you may discover that calm acceptance is possible. You relax because you are living in the present moment, not thinking about what happened ten minutes earlier or what will happen when you return to work. In this state of peace, it is easier to accept what is happening and respond to it from a place of inner calm.

Greg, the CEO of a large logistics company, was consumed by a desire for money, power, position, title, and the need to get ahead. You could say he completely became the suit he was wearing. He always thought he had to beat the guy next to him. All this fed his ego, and for a while it worked. But as he achieved success after success, the opposite began to occur. Instead of feeling satisfied, his ego only got hungrier. It was as if he was in a never-ending race that had no finish line, and yet he didn't stop to question what the point of making another million dollars was if he was just going to feel more disconnected from his children and wife.

Then Greg started to work with an executive coach and tap into his own purpose and heart. He decided to integrate this into his decision-making process. Together, Greg and the coach crafted a personal strategy that would give him fulfilment, joy and high levels of satisfaction. Not surprisingly, the things that fed his ego didn't even make the top ten items that he said brought him happiness. He discovered that what he loved most was to give, to delight people, and to create stories. Of course, he continued to focus on his business and creating wealth, but it was against a completely different backdrop—one driven by his internal world. In terms of the Life Journey Model, Greg was moving from the external to the internal arc, and integrating what he discovered in his internal world with his life in the external world.

In life, most suffering is linked to our obsession with things in the external world. That's why the external world arc in the model is lined with references to negative experiences. Similarly, lasting happiness tends to stem from the positive experiences that originate within ourselves. If you look at the model, you will see these positive experiences on the internal world arc. Of course, some degree of excitement and pleasure can be found in the external world, however, these experiences are not to be confused with *lasting* happiness as they are temporary in nature.

We tend to meet the challenges of the external world through a screen of fear and self-interest, which only leads to further pain and suffering. Among the challenges of the internal world are uncertainty and doubts. If we handle these through surrender and by following our intuition, they can turn into assets. When we accept that we can't and don't know what is going to happen, we open ourselves to the flowing possibility of all things.

It's really important that you do not fall into the trap of judging the external world as bad and the internal world as good. At any point during life, we may place greater emphasis on one world or the other; however, being able to live with both in balance is most desirable. Often, an accident, burnout, or another crisis occurring in the external world serves as a catalyst for a shift to occur. Through a process of awareness and healing, we are able to move from external to internal; from separation to oneness.

The model shows the two arcs growing farther apart because most people choose one arc. Most people choose to walk the external journey, and when they do, they forget to nurture their heart. As a result, the gap between their ego/suit and their heart/monk increases as time passes. Those people who listen to their heart and choose to follow their intuition decrease the gap. For them, the experience of a life based solely on ego becomes increasingly distant.

Keep in mind that although the model shows the external and internal worlds as opposites and oneness as the property of the internal world only, when we fully embrace the internal journey, these distinctions dissolve. In the state of oneness, instead of two arcs, the external and internal worlds are seen as integral parts of one whole.

The Model Describes Your Life

Every element in the model can be experienced in different "time zones" in your life. For example, even though happiness is shown at one point on the arc, it can be experienced at any age, whether you are young, middle-aged, or older. Similarly, unhappiness can be experienced at the beginning, middle, or end of your quest in the external world; again, it all depends on the journey you take.

You can use the model to help you understand your journey in life and the decisions you have made, as well as to help you make better decisions in the future. Joyce, whom you met in the

49

last chapter, felt she "woke up" when she saw the model. It confirmed to her that she had made the right choice in deciding not to leave her job. The model enabled her to realise that money alone was not the determining factor. She saw that money was on the external arc of her life, but what she valued more—being part of a community and having a sense of meaning and purpose—was a reflection of her internal world.

In the following chapters, you will see how to bridge the gap between your external and internal worlds, find greater peace, and discover your own path. You will also find explanations for the remaining elements of the model, such as acceptance/rejection, future/past, unconsciousness, and external wants and needs. You will learn how to apply these laws in your internal world to find happiness, meaning, love, purpose, and joy.

Chapter 4

The External Journey

4. The External Journey

The external journey is your journey in the world as you know it. It is the path you follow within the existing structures and boundaries of the particular society in which you live. You follow this path based on what you have learned, understood, and decided in your mind.

The External World

Depending on which part of the world and in which culture we were born, each of us carries within our genetic and psychological programming a specific set of ideas, beliefs, and judgements about what we *should* do in life. From an early age, we have specific ideas about what we need to *have* in order to find happiness.

Imagine if you were to tie a bird, a dog, a snake, a crocodile, and a monkey together with a rope. Each of these five animals would try to go back to its own home, using its own means. The snake would slither into the grass, the crocodile would crawl into the water, the bird would fly into the air, the dog would run to a village, and the monkey would climb a tree. However, we can't forget one important fact: the crocodile is the strongest and would probably drag all the rest with it into the water. Even though each animal has a different way of being in the world, in the end, they will all follow the same path.

Isn't this similar to what occurs in the external world today? The pressure of society to follow a certain life path—to have certain possessions and accomplish certain things—is like a powerful crocodile, pulling each individual toward the same predetermined goals and achievements. If you grew up in a family with enough money anywhere in the modern world, you were probably expected to get a college degree (or several) and find a job with compensation comparable to or higher than that of your peers. If you didn't do this, you wouldn't be called a success.

Even if you broke out of your native environment and lived in a different part of society, you have most likely only exchanged your original path for another established path. Instead of getting a law degree, for example, you might have set out to become an artist or a writer. Yet, even while you were doing something you loved, a new pressure to succeed may have arisen from the external world. Perhaps you started to think you had to sell a certain number of books or paintings in order to really "be someone". In the external world, you will always find someone who has more than you or who is more successful than you are.

Now, I don't mean to say these achievements of external success don't have their place. They do. Many such external accomplishments have transformed the world, changing and improving it for the benefit of many. The key point here is that what has brought others happiness may not necessarily bring *you* happiness. The security of a gated community may make one man feel like a king, but another like a prisoner.

The main challenge we face in the life journey is to become aware of our own path. This can only happen if we are in touch with our internal world and receive the guidance of our intuition. Yet most of us remain focused on the external world and rely exclusively on our rational mind. Most people today experience a large amount of suffering, pain, struggle, resistance, and frustration along their journey. They are unaware that they are following a path that is not their own. They're even less aware of the reasons they're on this path. What about you?

Whether we instinctively jump on the crocodile's back or try to resist, most of us still look to the external world for direction instead of listening to the CEO of life. We look to anything and everything outside of ourselves for answers: we read magazines, we watch TV, we talk to parents, friends and colleagues. "What do I need to do to be happy?" we ask. Everyone has a different answer: lose weight, upgrade your car, get married, change jobs. This is not surprising because we take everything in the external world to be real: the money, the car, the house, the job. Reality to our mind is whatever we can see, touch, smell, or taste. But nothing could be further from the truth. In fact we rarely, if ever, stop to search deep inside ourselves and ask, "What do *I* really want?", rather than what the crocodile is pulling us toward.

Nevertheless, most of us end up striving for external success in one form or another, trying to live up to others' and our own expectations. We think it is important to be liked, approved, and accepted, and to stand out as the best in the crowd, so we continue the struggle to get somewhere. Yet when it seems we have finally made headway, we're left wanting more. Sound familiar? The underlying feeling of not having enough, of emptiness, still lingers. Most people believe that someday they will arrive, that they will find a place where everything is settled, happy and at peace. But that arrival never happens.

Why do so many of us strive for external success when it ultimately fails to give us the fulfillment we're seeking? Again, most of us are simply unaware of our choices. It's as if we're living on autopilot. Most of us were conditioned early in life to associate certain outcomes with success. When we achieve such an outcome, we are praised. That praise only spurs us on to seek more recognition. First you start walking and your parents cheer you on; then you are awarded a prize for winning a race at school; then you receive praise for getting your diploma; then you are promoted at work and congratulated by your co-workers. The need to receive praise again and again is always there, and somehow you always feel you need more as this feeling of wanting never ends. Thus, from an early age, although we're not aware of it, most of us begin looking for external success. We think money, power, fame or status will bring us a state of freedom and happiness.

On the external journey, as people grow used to experiencing the high that comes from recognition and power, they direct their focus toward bigger and grander goals. They assume that these goals are their true life goals. Yet often these people are in for a rude awakening. We see this, for example, in some business people who have achieved many external successes. Others see these people as "having everything" and expect them to be happy. However, the truth is that they feel empty inside. They have forgotten or even consciously repressed the inner feeling of the here and now, that is, they are out of touch with what is happening in the present moment, right where they are, independent of past success or future goals. How happy are you in your work and life, really?

Of course, there is the rare person who is able to make a different choice. For example, I read about a marketing executive named John Wood, who left his position at Microsoft after trekking in Nepal on vacation. He visited a village school, where he saw that their library did not have a single book. So he felt moved to contact friends and colleagues online and arrange for books to be sent to the school. When he got home, he decided to quit his job and start a foundation, called Room to Read, dedicated to promoting literacy around the world. He gave up his financial security in the corporate world to do work he found more personally meaningful.

I'm not suggesting that the answer to the stress or disconnection you feel is to leave your corporate job. It's just that in today's society, we have been trained to accept strong feelings of stress, pain, anxiety, discomfort, and unhappiness in the now, in exchange for the expectation of what the future will bring. More and more people in the West take medications for depression, anxiety and other psychological disorders to cover up these feelings, rather than addressing the root of the problem. The root of all of these problems is not having a job in the business world; it is being disconnecting from one's inner self.

Over the past decade, researchers have reported that 50 percent of our happiness is determined by personality traits and genetics, and the other 50 percent by external factors such as relationships, health and careers. They refer to the hereditary component as our "happiness set point", implying that we aren't likely to achieve the level of happiness we might want. Not all researchers are quite so pessimistic. In *The How of Happiness*, University of California psychologist Sonja Lyubomirsky [8] concluded that even

---

8. Sonja Lyubomirsky, The How of Happiness: A Scientific Approach to Getting the Life You Want (New York: Penguin Press, 2007).

considering the happiness set point, at least 40 percent of our happiness is within our control. However, few of those attempting a scientific study of happiness take into consideration its true source: the inner self. The inner self is not influenced by genetics or by circumstance. As long as we focus on the external world, we will never have 100 percent control over our own happiness.

If we remain deeply unaware and repress our true inner desires in order to follow a path laid out for us externally, our journey will be full of struggle and discomfort. The source of this struggle is underlying conflict within one's self – wanting to be somewhere or do something in a place and time other than the here and now. But because we are unaware, we blame the struggle on other people or elements of the external world. Instead of feeling synergy (connection or alignment) within ourselves, we may accuse others of depriving us or standing in our way. This only serves to perpetuate the struggle, as we try harder to satisfy the desires that continually elude us.

The attachment we feel to the external world is extremely powerful and difficult to break away from once we've mentally identified ourselves with our goals and desires. When I was in the freight forwarding business, I mentally bought into the goals for success defined by my belief system. Every day was a struggle because I wasn't listening to my inner self. All I could hear was the voice of my ego.

The Ego

The *ego* is the aspect of us that identifies with our bodily form, possessions and personality. It is who we think we are. It is the label we put on ourselves. For example, it is the ego that says: "I am a man", "I am a woman", "I am a good person", "I am bad person", and so on.

The ego serves an important function in life. It is through the ego and the suit we wear that we express our differences, individuality, and uniqueness in the world and our work. Although the word *ego* often carries a negative connotation, truly speaking the ego and its suits are neither good nor bad; they are simply a human being's way of identifying himself or herself in the external world. Just as we are conditioned to think a certain way about what we should do and how we should live, in the external world, we also develop an identity from an early age, usually corresponding to our genetic makeup and environmental upbringing. A person learns to identify himself or herself as "I", which is separate from "you". This concept of the self exists as both the individual (e.g. "I am Johann, a 40-year-old mechanical engineer") and the collective (e.g. "I am German") levels.

To understand and strengthen the concept of "I", it is necessary to find and to focus on differences between "I" and "you". A child might say, "I have this toy, and you don't", thus indicating his or her separateness. In society today, children are commonly taught to think about themselves and others according to a perspective that emphasises differences: "I am Robbie and I am 12-years-old. I live in the city of Chicago, in the United States. My skin is white and I ride a red bike. You are Jenny and you are eight-years-old. Your skin is black, and you play netball". We believe that we are different; that we are separate people. We learn to see ourselves as separate people based on our external differences, as defined by our egos.

Because our ego or identification in the external world is born out of differences, the ego always needs a concept of "other" in order to thrive. To strengthen this mind-born sense of identity, the ego tends to judge itself in comparison with others: "I have this and you don't; I am this and you are not; I have more and you have less; I am better and you are worse". One's ego can grow when one gains success, money, and fame. Alternatively, one's ego can grow if one has less money but harbours a feeling of superiority over others.

Rich or poor, it is possible for anyone to have a big ego. This simply means one has a strong attachment to one's superficial image or suit, to their belongings, and to their external makeup, and that one derives one's sense of identity from these things. The ego need not be positive in order to be strong. An ego can arise in many shapes and forms, including a negative, victimised sense of self in which one believes one is inferior to others. Qualities such as shyness, self-consciousness, and feeling unworthy are among the many faces of the ego. The common denominator for all types of ego is a feeling of being different and separate from others.

For example, think of that guy at work who is always touting his achievements. It's all about "Look at me!", "Listen to me!", "Give it to me!" He has to speak first… and have the last word. He has to claim the best workstation, tell the most obnoxious jokes, and constantly push everyone else aside. It's easy to see his big ego, right? But then there is the guy who freezes up during presentations, avoids office parties, and complains that no one is supporting his project. When he begs you not to pick him to do any public speaking because he believes he'll have a meltdown if you do, you might be tempted into thinking, "this guy is so self-effacing, he must have no ego at all". But it's just the opposite: his ego *is* what makes him self-effacing. While the first guy's ego is about "I'm the greatest", the second's is all about "I'm the worst". It's the same song, just different melodies.

Psychologist Sandy Gluckman,[9] author of *Who's in the Driver's Seat: Using Spirit to Lead Successfully*, reports that as many as 63 percent of business people estimate that egotistical behaviour negatively affects work performance on a regular basis; more than half estimate it cuts company profit by as much as 15 percent.

I'm not suggesting you demolish your ego. The mental construct of ego is necessary for us to exist as a unique, individual personality in the sensory world. It's just that many people today have become so consumed with this outer identity that they've completely forgotten about being their authentic self in personal life and in their job. They are out of touch with the "being" within themselves—the aspect of themselves that existed even

---

9. Sandy Gluckman, "Business Team Building, Step 1: Recognizing How Ego Shows Up" (http//:sandygluckman.com, 2008).

before they were born and which is without conditioned behaviour or beliefs. They are functioning solely from an egotistical stance. As a matter of fact, the more people identify with things outside of themselves, the more disconnected they feel from their inner selves. If they derive their sense of identity from their car, their house, their designer bag, or their body, does it not come as a surprise that they experience so much anxiety and fear? These things in the external world are temporary and can change in a heartbeat. No wonder people feel afraid that they may lose their possessions, that things could change or be taken from them, or that they (and thus their sense of self) could be lost. What would they be without them?

Separation

In the Life Journey Model (Figure 1) you will find separation on the top left side. It is an experience that belongs to the external world. Because people are conditioned by society to think of themselves in terms of differences, they begin to feel deeply disconnected from themselves and others. A strong sense of separation between "I" and "you" and between "me" and "the world", leads people to feel inner emptiness or even fear of others and the outside world.

If you are born in the Middle East, your parents may follow the Islamic tradition and teach you in early childhood how to act as a Muslim. If you are born in Europe, your parents may follow the Judeo-Christian tradition and educate you in the corresponding belief system. If you are born in Tibet, your upbringing is likely to predispose you to follow Buddhism. All these respective teachings are based on where the individual was born. However, at birth we are all the same. The knowledge that we are different and separate is placed upon us after our birth, and is based on the beliefs, culture, and traditions of the external world into which we are born.

In the external world, our differences are apparent in our physical appearance, behaviour, background, education, and many other aspects, yet these variations are mostly learned; they are super-ficial differences based on our external journey and ego identi-fication. Although these differences obviously do exist, we tend to forget that we were all born naked and vulnerable into this world, and that we will ultimately all return to dust and to the same source. Throughout our journey, if we look deep within ourselves, we will find we have many of the same inher-ent values and desires in common. We all want to be happy and experience meaning in our lives.

Yet, in our daily lives most of us experience more feelings of separation than of sameness with others and the world around us. At work, we see our colleagues as different and separate. We say: "He is a sales manager. She is an accountant. He is a CEO". Most of the time, we find ourselves playing a role which is not aligned with who we really are on the inside. In effect, we feel separated from the people around us because our ego iden-tity creates a barrier between us, them, and the world. The ego is constantly fed by conflict and problems, and the sense of not having enough; thus, the more you identify with your ego and the external world, the more separation you feel between you and others, and ultimately from yourself. It is possible to recon-nect with others and the world around you. In the subsequent chapters, I will guide you through the journey of rediscovering this connection and becoming whole again in your life, as well as establishing authenticity in your work.

Wants and Needs to Satisfy Externally

The common mode of thinking in the modern world is still intimately identified with the ego. Because all things external have an expiration date, the ego is in constant search for its next fix. This can be a physical belonging, such as a car or pair of shoes; or it can be non-physical, such as winning an argument to prove oneself right or better than another. We all know from personal experience that the good feelings that follow such a supposed gain only last temporarily—in some cases, a mere instant—before we begin looking for something else we think will make us happy.

For example, think about the last physical object you purchased. Perhaps it was a bag, a piece of furniture, or an electronics item. You probably felt an initial good feeling or excitement when you bought it, but how long did that good feeling last? How long was it before you began thinking of your next purchase? Or think about the last time you were praised or recognised for an accomplishment. You probably felt great about yourself or at least about your ego identity, for example, "I am an outstanding employee". One area of your identity was strengthened which you felt good about, but undoubtedly the feeling did not deeply penetrate other areas of your life or last for long.

Again, the point is not to say that egoic wanting is good or bad. What we need to realise is that it inevitably results in a feeling of insufficiency when the ego realises it has not been fully satisfied by the external thing or response. It is a truism that money doesn't make you happy. Researchers have even proven this. In one well-known study conducted in 1978,[10] psychologists compared a group of people who had won the Illinois state lottery and received up to a million dollars with a second group of victims who had been paralysed in horrible accidents. They also included a third group, selected at random from the phone book. The researchers interviewed all their subjects and found the lottery winners were not happier than the members of the other groups; in fact, the winners took less pleasure in routine daily activities than the other groups. Interpreting these findings, Harvard University psychologist Daniel Gilbert[11] said people consistently misjudge the extent of pleasure they will experience when their egoic wants are satisfied. Have you ever desired a job promotion for years, finally gotten it, felt really excited, and then after a couple of months the satisfaction was gone?

10. Elizabeth Kolbert, "Everybody Have Fun: What Can Policymakers Learn from Happiness Research?" New Yorker Magazine (2010, March 22).

11. Daniel Gilbert, Stumbling on Happiness (New York: Knopf, 2006).

Advertising relies on the insistent demands of egoic wanting. Many commercials claim that when we have acquired x, y, or z we will be happy or feel better. Though that might be true, the happiness or good feeling is only temporary. Our drive to consume things in the external world has been conditioned so effectively that our behaviour as a consumer has become completely unconscious. Most of us don't stop to question for what purpose we need something or what we will really gain from it. Of course, this is not our fault; it's just how we have been raised. We fully believe that more is better and that when we get what we think we want, we shall be satisfied and fulfilled. Yet in the end, our satisfaction always turns out to be only temporary.

A few years ago, researchers [12] attempted to draw a "map of happiness" across England, Scotland, and Wales, and identify the communities where people were most and least happy. They also took into consideration factors such as employment and how long people had lived in a particular area. One conclusion from the study was that people who were unemployed tended to be, on average, happier if they lived in an area of high unemployment than if they lived some place where everyone around them had a job. I found this interesting because it demonstrates clearly how people look to the external environment not only to measure how happy they feel in their lives but also to determine how happy they believe they can be.

The Cycle of Pleasure and Pain

So why does the external journey ultimately turn out to be unfulfilling?

The answer lies in the temporary nature of the external world. When we attach our happiness to something in the external world and the external world changes, our happiness changes

---

12. Matt McGrath, "Britain's Happiest Places Mapped" BBC News (2008, 28 August).

too. Although we might have thought it would last, it doesn't. It is simply replaced by a new desire for something else. In trying to find a way to sustain our fleeting moments of happiness, we end up in an endless cycle of happiness and unhappiness. It is important we recognise that this kind of happiness differs significantly from true happiness.

For example, when I was working in Shenzhen, China, I would feel happy when I got a new client or made a sale. I would go home that evening feeling relaxed. However, my happiness inevitably faded when the newness of the success had passed, if a new problem arose or if the pressure to achieve a goal intensified. In comparison, the true happiness I felt after awakening was deep and unshakeable.

When we feel fleeting happiness, what we experience is merely a rush of excitement. It is actually a sensation of pleasure. Pleasure is only a temporary reaction to our surroundings; it should not be mistaken for true happiness. I don't mean to imply that pleasure is a bad thing. Pleasure is fine if it can be experienced along with true happiness. If you become whole as a person and then add the experience of pleasure, you will still be happy once the pleasure is over. For example, if I am content within myself before getting dressed up and going out to dinner with friends, I will enjoy the event while it lasts, and when it is over I will still be equally content within myself.

You may have been advised to remind yourself about happiness by reading books or by repeating positive affirmations about what you appreciate in your life. These techniques can uplift you and generate feelings of happiness, however, once again, they are only temporary solutions. A few hours after you repeat an affirmation, chances are the happiness it induced will have faded. You will be caught in a cycle of needing to continually repeat and refresh the affirmation in order to sustain happiness. Any happiness that you must make an effort to achieve is not true happiness.

Most of us are familiar with the ups and downs that come with the cycle of pleasure and pain. For example, the pleasure derived from drinking alcohol or taking drugs one day turns to an equivalent sensation of pain the next. The extreme high experienced while completely infatuated and consumed by another person can quickly turn to loathsome anger when he or she is no longer there to give you that feeling. Thrill seekers engage in dangerous acts to experience pleasure and participants often admit these activities to be addictive, causing them to continually seek the next high or chase after the rush.

The more you feel compelled to seek temporary pleasure on the outside, the more likely you are to experience pain. Of course, you may be able to enjoy any specific pleasure without needing to repeat it—it is possible to enjoy one ice cream cone without needing to rush out and buy another or to go skydiving without needing to do it again. However, when you come to the point of realising that what you are really seeking can't be found in all of these external things, it is common to experience deep unhappiness. This happens to many people when they reach midlife and realise that what they have been pursuing was not their true destination.

Now What?

If you are becoming aware that you want something more fulfilling than the temporary happiness the external world has to offer, this realisation in and of itself is the first step toward discovering lasting happiness.

In the following chapter we shall discover in greater detail where deep feelings of unhappiness and emptiness come from and how to begin to transform them into happiness, fulfillment, and joy.

Chapter 5

The Gap

5. The Gap

When I am leading a workshop, I ask people, "What matters to you in life?" They respond by saying things such as love, care, and friendship. So then I ask them to consider a situation in which they did not act in accordance with what they believe matters most.

For example, suppose you say honesty is important, but then you think of a situation in which a shopkeeper gave you too much change and you didn't say, "You gave me too much". On the one hand, you felt good because you got more change, but on the other hand, you were uncomfortable because you knew in your heart you were not doing the right thing.

In a situation such as this, where you know you didn't do the right thing, a Gap is created. Your mind feels good about the extra change, but your heart feels uncomfortable. In between the heart and the mind is a feeling of discomfort.

Take another example. An older person is standing next to you on the bus and you don't give up your seat, even though you feel you should because you maintain values of generosity, compassion, and respect. A Gap is created. A person who did not share those values and who did not give up his seat would not experience a Gap in that instance, however, because you do hold these values, giving up your seat is the most aligned action. The Gap is only created by a discrepancy between thought and feeling; heart and mind.

You can think of the Gap like a container of water. Every time you take an action in which you are not true to yourself, water is added to the container. Sometimes you're only adding two or three drops of water to the container at a time, for instance, by not giving up your seat on the bus. Other times you can add a litre or more to the container, through negative experiences such as a divorce or getting fired. The more water you carry around, the heavier the container, the bigger the burden you feel, and the more you suffer.

What you need is a mechanism to continuously empty the container.

One of my coaching clients is a man who lives in Shanghai. He is married with a child, has a house in Europe, is very successful in his career, and generally enjoys a good life. Nevertheless, he feels deeply unhappy and a long way away from living the life he truly desires. At one point, he told me his inner pain was so extreme that he was considering suicide. Here is a man who apparently has everything life could offer, yet is so unhappy that he wants to give up his life altogether. How is this possible?

It is possible because a Gap has been created. His external and internal worlds have become so separated that it is as if he has fallen into a huge crevice between the two. We all have a Gap to a certain extent. Maybe it is not as extreme as the example I just mentioned, but feelings of unhappiness or not being fully satisfied are manifested in most of us. Let's look at how this Gap is created within you, and how you can close it.

How the Gap is Created

You're not born with a Gap. When you observe young children, most are curious, fearless, and have seemingly unlimited energy. As long as they are well fed and feel loved and secure, they have no anxiety. Their experience is one of complete absorption in whatever they are doing, and they are very good at living in the present moment. From a child's perspective, there is no past and future, just what is happening now.

You may not remember your earliest years clearly, but try to think back. Did you feel a sense of stress, anxiety, unhappiness, or worries about life? If your parents were there to take care of you, those were probably carefree years. Before we begin to grow up and wider society starts to have a stronger influence, the spirit that is born into this world is very free.

Then as you get a bit older, you begin to realise you have an individual self. You become aware you have a name. You learn your parents are "Mum" and "Dad", and that they are separate people from you and from each other. You don't always want to do what they tell you to do, so you learn you can say "No!" You enjoy playing with toys, but you also discover that a toy is separate from you. If another child wants to play with your teddy bear, you resist, you become selfish. "It's mine!" you cry. If you are asked to share, it may not have been easy at first because an attachment has been created to the teddy bear. You don't want to give it up because it gives you pleasure and happiness, and you don't want to risk losing that pleasure. Your desire is to make the source of your happiness—in this case the teddy bear—permanent. This attachment is a form of delusion because nothing in life is permanent.

As you grow up, a teddy bear becomes a bicycle, then clothes, a car, a house, a relationship, a job and so on. You look more and more to the external to give you a sense of pleasure or satisfaction. You are reluctant to let others get too close to that source of pleasure because that might mean less for you; your ego doesn't like that idea.

Career success, identification with the egoic self, the need and desire to have things, the search for pleasure—all these collectively drive your focus toward things in the external world. This is normal because it's how we are conditioned as we grow up, however, there is a huge downside. When your focus is on the external world, you become increasingly disconnected from your true self, true desires, and purpose in life.

You see this often in the workplace. You may be so consumed with the desire to have a certain job or buy a certain car that the journey to get there becomes simply a means to an end. You feel you must get what you want at any cost because you believe the achievement of your objective will give you lasting happiness. You forget that the pursuit of this objective might bring high levels of stress from working extreme hours and giving up all your free time. In turn, what you feel in your heart,

71

your true inner desire, is ignored or pushed aside in exchange for the promise of a future outcome in the external world. Your happiness then becomes dependent on that future outcome, whether it is a job promotion; money; or a physical object, such as a car or a house.

In sum, the way you are brought up predisposes you to experience the Gap. From an early age, your parents, teachers, and society in general place so much focus on the external world that a Gap is created between your inner self, and the part of you that longs for and feels it cannot live without an increasing number of possessions and accomplishments. I'm not saying it is bad to be successful or have a lot of money. This is fine if it comes from following your true purpose and not from trying to feed a hungry ego. If you find your true purpose first—what you love to do, what you are born to do—and then make money out of accomplishing your purpose, no Gap will be created between your self and the ego.

Of course, it would be ideal if parents were to teach their young children to look within themselves. Unfortunately, few parents know how to do this. As a result, most of us grow up closing ourselves off in a box defined by fear and other negative tendencies of the ego. This is our world as we know it today. It would also be ideal if people received help and encouragement in the workplace to discover their inner self and to find purpose and meaning which they could express in their jobs to create better relationships with their colleagues.

Public Examples of the Gap

I find it can be interesting and helpful to speculate how the Gap has manifested in certain people's lives. You will be familiar with some of the individuals I describe here because of their public personas. Use them as models to better understand how the Gap operates in your life.

Anita Roddick was an English businesswoman who founded The Body Shop in 1976. She was an entrepreneur and was passionate about her business. From the beginning she wanted to provide women with quality products that promoted not only beauty but health and well-being. She strived to make her company a model of ethical business practices and value-based leadership. As an activist, she led campaigns against animal testing and was in support of community trade. She worked to promote the self-esteem of her customers, to defend human rights, and to protect the environment. She once said, "There is no scientific answer for success. You can't define it. You've simply got to live it and do it." As such, it is likely she is an example of someone with a small or nonexistent Gap.

Firemen who risk their lives over and over to save those of others also have little or no Gap. A fire chief by the name of Bob Lewis, who worked for the Fire Department in the small town of Hardeeville, South Carolina, USA, once said: "A fireman who says he is never afraid is either a fool or not a fireman". In other words, a fire fighter is a real human being with real human emotions, but because he is in touch with his purpose, he is able to perform heroic acts.

On the other hand, take the example of Whitney Houston. Although she was a talented and highly successful singer, Whitney suffered from bouts of self-doubt that led her to depend on drugs, which ultimately contributed to her tragic death. Other famous celebrities, such as Michael Jackson and Amy Winehouse, provide similar examples. In each case, the individual seems to have everything one could possibly desire, yet lasting happiness eludes them. This may seem incomprehensible, especially to those of us who don't know fame firsthand, but we have to understand that it is the Gap within such individuals that causes them trouble.

In each of us, it is the Gap that determines how we feel. It doesn't matter how successful you are, how famous you are, or how poor you are, the way you manage your Gap makes all the difference when it comes to your experience of happiness or unhappiness.

Suffering and Negative Emotions

Pain and suffering are caused by our decision to give meaning, purpose, and value to the external world. For example, you may be so attached to your car that if someone scratches it, even by accident, you feel as if you, personally, have been "scratched". This happens because your ego is projected onto the car as a means of gaining status and value in the external world. Similarly, if a friend criticises something you have done, you feel hurt because you think they have rejected not just your behaviour, but everything about you.

We may try to persuade ourselves that we don't have to suffer, but that doesn't necessarily stop us from suffering. The Gap that has been created between our true self and the ego makes us continue to suffer.

Fear, anger, and grief are emotions associated with the ego. Fear keeps many of us from moving forward in life. We are held back by fears of failure, rejection, and loss. As I mentioned in chapter 3, the ego will reject anything that makes it feel uncomfortable. These negative emotions keep us tied to the external world and are the result of the ego's identification with events or circumstance. We experience anger and fear when the ego feels threatened. In the face of threat, we blame other people, places or things we feel are causing us grief, but in reality the cause of suffering is our own attachment to those people, places or things. In the words of Sophocles, "The greatest griefs are those we cause ourselves".[13]

Emotions are food for the brain. Negative emotions create repetitive patterns of thinking and feeling that are hard to break. These patterns can poison our lives in many ways. Once these negative patterns of thinking and feeling become ingrained, our self-image is affected. Whatever we think and feel, we become. The more you are focused on judgements and interpretations, the more emotions you will experience-negative or positive.

---

13. John 16:13, King James Bible, New American Standard Version (1995).

Being smart in the external world means having a good education and a degree, right? This belief caused negative emotions in me and affected my life in many ways as I was never academically inclined. I told myself that I wasn't qualified for certain jobs and that the people around me were much smarter. For example, when our company had a high-potential programme, I made the assumption that the people in it must be really smart. Later on, after I had been invited to become part of it, I still believed I was not smart. This affected my self-image and I became deferential when communicating with others. Some people acknowledged my talent, but I told myself they were lying to me.

People in the business environment suffer and feel negative emotions when they don't enjoy what they are doing. Every morning they hate to wake up and go to the office. For them, every action in life feels like a struggle.

At a certain point, suffering becomes a habit. Knowing we will suffer gives us at least some degree of certainty. We are familiar with what is going to happen, and that familiarity creates a sense of safety. We want to feel safe even if it means we will continue to suffer. Suffering happens to each and every one of us and if we run away from it, it will hunt us down until we have the courage to face it.

I was once asked if life can exist without problems, challenges, or suffering. I answered yes. My mind told me at that time it was not possible, but my monk was experiencing it. Now I can see that it is not that difficult to eliminate suffering. By embracing your inner monk and walking your internal journey, sooner or later your suffering will diminish.

Caught in the Gap

Do you recognise the Gap in your own life?

You may experience it as pain, as a feeling of emptiness, or as deep dissatisfaction. It is as though you're living in a void, an empty space, a place of "not enough". Of course, there are times where you feel good and happy for a while because something in the external world has happened that is pleasing to you. Those events are temporary in nature. Inevitably the pleasure wears off and the feeling of being in the Gap returns. You can probably think of a few times in your life when this has happened. Being aware of the existence of your Gap means you are aware of the conflict between your suit and your monk.

SUIT	MONK
Your name (John, Jane)	Your heart (no name)
Your work	Your purpose
Dependent	Independent
Demanding/receiving	Giving
Over/under-confident	Confident

Figure 2 illustrates the relationship between your internal and external worlds. The outer line and the area beyond that line represent your ego and social identity, or the suit you wear in the world. This includes your job, money, your car, the house you live in, the clothes you wear, and so on. At the centre of the diagram is your true self or inner monk. Most people experience a Gap between these two, to a greater or lesser degree.

Figure 2. Relationship Between the Internal and External Worlds

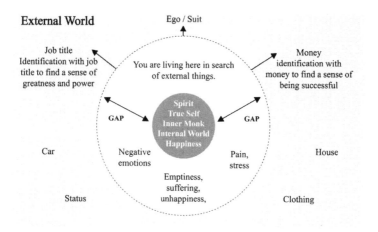

It may not be obvious at first, but the Gap can become larger or smaller depending on the choices you make. As you read the rest of this book, you will find all the information you need to make choices that can reduce that Gap.

Many of us do not pay much attention to the Gap because we assume it will automatically close whenever we get the external objects we crave. We figure the discomfort caused by the Gap is just a temporary inconvenience to be endured. For example, you may think, "I'll be happy when I get that new car", and for a short period that's true. Remember, happiness that comes from anything in the external world is temporary. Similarly, while you wait for the desired object to arrive, you extend the possibility of being happy as you believe that happiness is just over the horizon or just around the corner, and that you'll achieve it sooner or later.

Mastery of the Gap applies to organisations as well as individuals. You may have worked in an organisation where great emphasis was placed on goals, targets, performance, and all the demands of the external world. A certain amount of success and achievement is possible in this kind of environment. However, if you work in an organisation that nurtures the inner worlds of its employees by paying attention to meaning, purpose, and engagement, you will respond with far greater energy and commitment than someone who works in an organisation which does not.

Fortunately, it is possible to close the Gap in your work and life and to bring your internal and external worlds into alignment. Using the Gap model, this can be done in three basic ways. However, before I introduce these ways, it will be helpful to consider two important laws: the law of rejection and the law of acceptance. When you understand how these laws operate in your life, it will be easier to bridge your Gap.

Chapter 6

The Laws Of Rejection And Acceptance

6. The Laws of Rejection and Acceptance

When divers are underwater, they take great precaution to make sure they are safe. This includes diligent monitoring of their air supply, which is vital to their survival. If they ever become aware of a problem, it is essential that they do not panic as panicking will cause a rapid loss of oxygen, and potentially put their lives in jeopardy. In fact, they are a taught a procedure to help guard against panic. A diver has to accept the situation, focus on slowing his breathing rate, and stay calm. In this way, he loses less oxygen and can resolve the underlying problem much faster.

You could say the same applies in everyday life. When you encounter a crisis or a situation you don't like, your tendency may be to reject what is happening and go into denial about it. This is like the diver whose panic wastes precious oxygen. Instead you want to stay calm. If you start by accepting whatever is happening, whether or not you like it, you observe the event without giving meaning to it. In this state of mind, you can hear the voice of your inner monk more easily, which can then help you find the best solution.

At the end of the day, we cannot control what will happen to us in life, but we are able to choose the way in which we respond, and that in turn will determine if we are happy or if we suffer. In this chapter, we will look at the laws of rejection and acceptance and at how these laws relate to whether we experience happiness or unhappiness.

The Law of Rejection

Did you ever become angry when someone took something you wanted for yourself? Did you ever react emotionally when someone criticised you? Have you ever felt frustrated because you didn't get a promotion or job offer from a company? Have you ever felt resentful when a relationship ended? If the answer is yes, you may have inadvertently applied the law of rejection to yourself.

Rejection is the foundation for unhappiness. The law of rejection can be expressed as follows: whenever we reject something—whether it is an external situation or an internal feeling, a negative past emotion or state—we increase the Gap between our true self and the ego; the heart and the mind; the suit and the monk. Whenever we reject or resist our current situation, we experience more pain and suffering.

Many undesirable and unforeseen events happen in life. We like to think we have control over ourselves and over these situations. This makes us feel safe, stable, and powerful. We may feel a sense of security and safety, but we don't really have the degree of control we think we have. We resist and we reject in an effort to gain and maintain control, but our efforts are in vain. Like most of us who are creatures of habit and comfort, you undoubtedly have learned to reject these changes. Even if opportunities accompany these events, you fear change and so you reject it. As a result, you maintain or even increase the Gap within you.

A woman I met recently told me she had been a high achiever her whole life. The drive and need for success had consumed her. Even though her body was asking her to slow down, she had continued to reject those messages until she became ill. Her face was tense and her lips were trembling as she shared her story. "I tried so hard to live up to others' expectations", she said. "But no matter what I did, I was never good enough". I could sense her fragility; it seemed as though she might break any minute. She thought her actions would please others, but what she had really been doing was rejecting her own self. As long as she continued to ignore her body's message which came in the form of chronic illness, it seemed unlikely she would heal.

Rejection tends to be based on deep-seated fear. As we move along in the life journey we have an internal drive to learn, evolve, and change; however, our mind has become identified with the status quo and thus we fear losing what we have (Figure 3). For example, if you don't get the promotion you hoped for, you may feel pain and frustration because you think your ego identity is in question. You fear that you are somehow less in the eyes of others and of yourself. If you think, "I don't want this to be happening", you will probably feel even more upset and frustrated. In fact, your focus on the undesired and fearful external situation increases and actually reinforces the status quo.

Rejection can result from negative past emotions that were never resolved. For example, the loss of a person who passed away, a divorce from which you never recovered, or a former colleague with whom you are still angry. Any negative event you hold onto resides within the Gap. For instance, I experienced the Gap when I was unable to forgive my father for leaving me during my teenage years.

Rejection also happens on the level of personal identity. For example, when someone says something bad or negative about you at work you automatically take it personally and react. You may become defensive because you think you will be and feel less worthy if you don't. You are uncomfortable with what the person has said, but even more uncomfortable with the idea of not responding. In this way, you sustain the Gap within you.

Figure 3. Rejection Increases the Gap

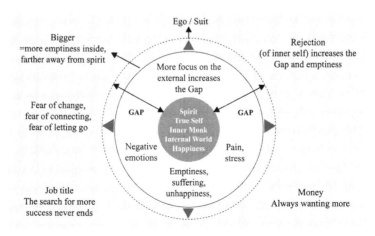

83

Often it is not a matter of outright rejection. It can be more subtle than that. Instead of a flat "No!", you simply put up resistance. It's like erecting a wall around yourself, as that resistance can continue for a long time and become your prevailing attitude. The more you resist the messages that come to your suit (i.e. from the external world), the larger the Gap you will experience and the more you will suffer. This won't just create problems for you, it can make things difficult for the people around you. They may find it hard to like and accept you if you are continuously blaming them for your situation. Nor will people appreciate you if you have built a wall around yourself that keeps them out. Someone you may perceive as authoritarian may actually be living within their own Gap and not know how to overcome it. Such people are not bad, they just have created a Gap and become stuck in it. Do you know someone—for example, a boss, friend, or even spouse—who can come across as overly controlling, inflexible, defensive, or resistant? Or perhaps even yourself? Whoever it might be, take the time to dig below the surface and understand the reason for the behaviour.

When we live in the external world, our problems and challenges are often due to the ego's need for attention and gratification. We tend to talk about other people's faults or point out how situations are not right for us. It's always "them" (an external factor) that make us feel the way we feel. In the external world we act as if we are the victim of others, and even of ourselves.

You see, even though the ego may appear to be threatened by anything that doesn't go its way, its goal is to keep pursuing people or things to challenge. The ego actually thrives on challenge and conflict, and does not object when negativity such as anger, fear, aggression, and depression, arises. Of course, we think we don't like challenges and we spend a lot of time worrying about what could go wrong when encountering them, but even that worry is food to the ego. All of this leads us to become further mired in the Gap.

Before we turn to the law of acceptance, take a moment to examine how the law of rejection manifests in your life. Here are some relevant questions:

- Are there aspects of yourself you don't like?
- When you make a mistake or something doesn't go the way you want, are you self-critical or self-accepting?
- What do you tell yourself when you are being self-critical?
- How do you feel (e.g. happy, anxious) when you are self-critical?

The Law of Acceptance

You may be wondering how you can overcome resistance and rejection, and how you can bridge the Gap within yourself. One prerequisite step is to become acquainted with and embrace the law of acceptance.

The law of acceptance states that whenever we accept something—whether it is an external situation or an internal feeling or state—we decrease the Gap (Figure 4). Because we can't control the external world, the wisest approach is to accept what happens to us. By acceptance, I don't mean giving up or becoming passive, I mean recognising that the event or circumstance "is what it is", without resisting it or attributing additional meaning to it. In fact, it can involve taking an active stance and facing what is happening without judgement, and simply welcoming it.

Years ago when I was learning to swim, someone I met at the beach advised me to always stand facing the waves and dive into them, rather than turning my back and letting them push me over so my face ends up in the sand. I like this metaphor because it helps you to understand the law of acceptance. The ocean waves symbolise our emotional issues, or what we fear from the external world. Most people turn their back to them thinking they will somehow avoid being knocked down, but the waves strike them down again and again.

The solution is to face the wave and dive into it. Yes, you will feel a little turbulence when you hit the wave, but the water will carry you until the wave breaks on the shore and disappears into the sand. Similarly, when you dive into an emotion you will feel a little turbulence, but if you embrace it fully, the emotion will go through you and disappear. You will feel light and peaceful within, which comes from accepting rather than resisting.

Figure 4. Acceptance Decreases the Gap

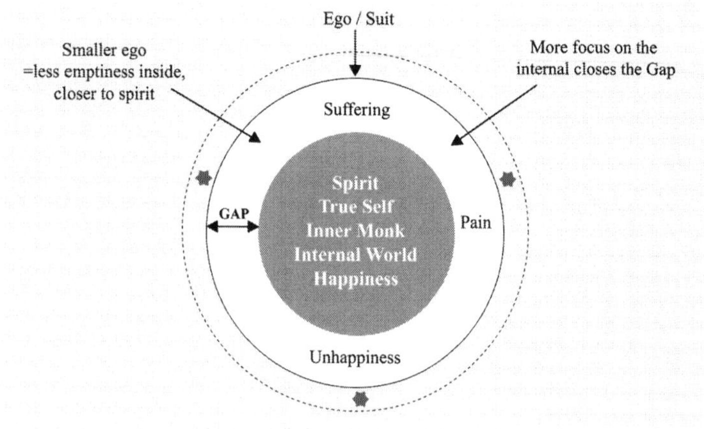

To get a firsthand experience of the difference between resisting and accepting, try this small, simple exercise. Take your shoes off and walk on your bathroom floor or on any cold stone or tiled flooring. Unless it's a hot day, your first reaction will probably be the feeling of dislike as your feet touch the cold floor. Your initial feeling might be to remove your feet right away, but hold on! Instead of resisting the unpleasant sensation, stay there and allow your feet to absorb the cold. See if you notice a change after a few moments. Your feet will still feel cold, but it is likely you will experience less discomfort. The cold remains the same, but the way your body reacts to it is different.

This easy exercise might not sound like a big deal but you can practice the same principle in other situations that have more real-life impact. For example, the next time you accidentally spray coffee on your shirt, wait a moment! Sure, you might feel angry with yourself but before you get too upset, try accepting what has already happened. If you like, you can do a little experiment. First try telling yourself, "That stupid coffee! My shirt is ruined!" and see how you feel. Now try changing the way you speak to yourself, for example, "Okay, I have spilled my coffee. I can accept that". See if you feel different.

Something like this happened recently when I hired an intern for my office. On her first day, we gave her a new laptop to start work, and two hours later she accidentally spilled a cup of water on it. Of course, the laptop was ruined. She had a choice to either accept what happened and move on, or reject it and beat herself up about it. Fortunately, we made a joke about it, and she was able to resume work after a short time, feeling at peace.

In fact, following the law of acceptance can dramatically alter your experience and determine whether you will suffer in life or become more at peace within. One example comes from Maria, a young woman who participated in a workshop and who later sent an email to tell me she was sick and had to have an operation. After the surgery, she continued to experience many symptoms. Maria said: "For the first time ever in my life, I experienced many different types of pain in my body. Surprisingly, I ENJOYED the pain very much, although some of it came from a horrible situation. Because I realised how badly I had treated my body for quite a long period of time, I was happy giving my body a chance to complain. I had a deep conversation with my body, and with my soul".

Accept Challenges

Sometimes life brings us challenges in big ways, and sometimes in smaller ways. Each challenge is an opportunity for growth. While we can't escape what is happening now, in the future, or in the past, we can change how we respond. In each moment we have an opportunity to either resist or accept. Another way to look at this is to say that we can either become a victim or take ownership. When I say "ownership", I mean owning who you are, what you stand for, and what you believe in. Thus, practising acceptance is a source of spiritual strength.

I'll give a small example from my own life. A few years ago, I signed up to give a presentation at a TEDx event in Taiwan. I had eight days to prepare, so I stopped all my business activities because I wanted everything to be perfect. This was my chance to share my ideas with the world! When the day arrived, I was nervous, but the first five minutes went well. Then I gave the signal to turn on the PowerPoint. Nothing! Their computer had crashed. There I stood, in front of 120 people, with nothing to say. It was a challenge I hadn't anticipated. What to do? I started laughing and told the audience, "Everything in life happens for a reason. I'm not sure what the reason for this is, but—" Everyone laughed. They thought it was part of my presentation. I even said, "If someone knows a good joke, please come on stage".

Even though the talk had this hiccup, I suddenly saw the joy and fun of it. I saw how foolish I had been to put so much pressure on myself and simply let go. In that moment, I had a choice: I could either become upset and respond negatively or I could accept the situation and embrace and learn from what was happening.

Today this is how I live my life whenever challenges arise, large or small. If I miss out on a business opportunity, I accept it. If I put all my efforts, resources, and talent into something and it doesn't work, I accept that and move on. Maybe the project was not meant to be mine, or maybe a competitor simply offered better value. If an issue arises in a relationship with loved ones or colleagues, I accept it; face it; and together with them, find the best possible solution.

We all encounter challenges, have to make choices in our day-to-day lives, and occasionally make mistakes. It is how we perceive our challenges that makes all the difference. As M. Scott Peck said, "Life is difficult. This is a great truth, one of the greatest truths. It is a great truth because once we truly see this truth, we transcend it. Once we truly know that life is difficult—once we truly understand and accept it—then life is no longer difficult. Because once it is accepted, the fact that life is difficult no longer matters".[14]

One man who took my workshop very much wanted to join the US Army as a combat medic; however, the maximum enlistment age had recently dropped from forty-two to thirty-five. Although he intended to apply for an age waiver, he thought he would most likely be denied because he was forty-one. He said, "It will be a disappointment if I am denied because of my age, but I will accept it and continue with my life, knowing the universe has a plan for me. Being receptive, I know good things will come". I never found out whether he was accepted or not, but I could see he was at peace with whatever the outcome might be.

Write a Letter

Accepting what happened in the past and letting it go allows you to release yourself from past experiences or events, including wrinkles in your relationships. For example, if you had an argument with a former boss or friend, you may want to write him or her a letter as a way to show you accept what happened and have let it go. You may or may not want to mail the letter, it doesn't matter. Either way, this action will free your mind from the burden of resistance.

When you accept everything that happens around you, you open yourself up to more possibilities along the journey of life. By writing a letter to your friend and fully accepting what happened between you, you open a door to new ways of relating to each other. I've even heard of instances in which one person accepted what had happened in a past relationship and the other person responded by reaching out to them—even when the first person did not tell the second person about that change of heart. The freedom gained from acceptance is so powerful that it can transform all aspects of your life and the lives of those you love.

---

14. M. Scott Peck, The Road Less Traveled, (New York: Touchstone, 2003), 15

You may also wish to write a letter of gratitude to a person in your life whom you have never properly thanked before. Often we have family members, colleagues or former bosses who give us a lot of support but we haven't properly thanked. Write a letter of gratitude and tell them specifically what you appreciate about them. They may or may not respond, however, that is not the point. By expressing your gratitude, you have deepened your own acceptance of your life journey.

The more you practise the law of acceptance in your daily life, the more you can experience a sense of complete freedom. Each challenge, hiccup, or wrinkle is simply an invitation for growth. By practicing acceptance, you come to realise that a challenge itself won't defeat you. Instead, it becomes a source of inner strength and happiness and a way to build self-confidence. When you accept a situation, you move closer to your true self—which is the source of true happiness—and allow yourself to respond more appropriately by setting a clearer course of action. You lose less energy and experience fewer negative emotions as the Gap becomes smaller. The Polish-American pianist Arthur Rubinstein said, "There is no formula for success, except perhaps an unconditional acceptance of life and what it brings".

Try practising the law of acceptance for a few weeks and see if you notice a significant decrease in the Gap within you and an increase in happiness.

Chapter 7

Closing The Gap

7. Closing The Gap

Practicing the law of acceptance is the first step in closing the Gap between your external and internal worlds, between your suit and your monk. This chapter includes more practical exercises to help you work with closing your own Gap. It is a very full chapter, so allow yourself time to work through it at a pace that is comfortable to you.

You have two people on your team to help you on your journey: your suit and your monk. It is up to you to decide which you would like to call in for help, and when. It can be hard to choose between your suit and your monk because both have solutions to offer. For example, when you want to change a job, your suit may help you work out the best way forward in a practical sense. But your monk will also have some available insight to bring to the conversation. It works best when you can interact with both your suit and your monk and have them work together as a team, generally with input from your monk coming first.

Sometimes the voice of the suit will be the dominant voice; for example, if you need to work out how to manage your pension programme, your monk will have very little to contribute. If you want to find the love of your life, on the other hand, you can't give that to the suit. You have to put your faith in something else, and your monk is your best guide. Choosing a new home is often a decision that requires input from both your suit and your monk, because your home will affect the quality of your daily life for many years. It has to feel right and also has to meet your logistical, financial, and practical needs. It is safe to say that most decisions should be done jointly, with the input from your monk coming first.

Measuring Your Gap

Before you attempt to close the Gap, it is helpful to get a better sense of how your Gap is currently manifested. Figure 5 shows a personal Gap model that illustrates how I would have responded a few years ago to the types of questions seen below. Responses (a) through (d) illustrate my Gap, arising from feelings and beliefs related to my interactions in the external world at that time. Responses (e) through (h) are issues from the past I had not resolved within myself and that contributed to the creation of my Gap.

Examine this diagram and then read the questions that follow and see how they apply in your life.

Figure 5. Personal Gap Model

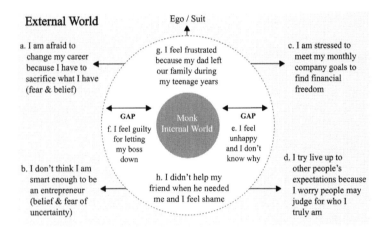

1. First consider how you interact in your suit with the external world.

   a. What fears are holding me back in life?
   b. What beliefs do I hold about why I can't do something?
   c. What do I feel frustrated about in life?
   d. What do I feel bothered about in the external world?

2. Next consider how effectively you manage your emotions and feelings.

   e. Do I understand why I feel as I do in my day-to-day life?
   f. Is there anything I feel guilty about in my life?
   g. Do I have negative emotions about my past that I have not resolved?
   h. Is there anything which I feel ashamed about?

3. Finally, consider how and when you take time to listen to and nurture your inner monk. Read each of the following statements and try it on for size. How accurately does it describe you in your current day-to-day life?

- I have accepted myself completely.
- I am true to my inner self when I make decisions, even if friends, family, or peers do not approve.
- I know and follow my purpose in life.
- I listen to my gut feelings and intuition.
- I regularly take personal time to nurture myself.
- I am comfortable with ambiguity.
- I have trust and faith that all will work out well.

Now that you have done your own self-assessment, do you have a better overall sense of the extent to which the Gap manifests in your life? If all the statements in part 3 currently ring true, you are probably comfortable with yourself and have learned how to deal with the external and internal worlds in an optimal way. Your Gap most likely is quite minimal. On the other hand, if you feel controlled by the feelings in part 1 and do not have solutions in part 2 that work well for you, your Gap needs to be closed. When you are able to close it, you will find greater happiness and peace within.

Three Methods to Close the Gap

The three methods you can use to close the Gap correspond to the three areas you just measured yourself in.

1. Change how you interact in your suit with the external world
2. Effectively manage your emotions and feelings
3. Take time regularly to listen to and nurture your inner monk

Common to all three is that they show you how to work from the inside out, coming from a place beyond the mind. This is the main way to close the Gap. When you place less emphasis on the suit or the ego, you automatically feel less emptiness and feel closer to your inner monk.

Each of these approaches involves practice. This is true just as it is for any form of physical exercise that must be practiced. When the muscle of your inner self is exercised and strengthened, it transforms from a weak spiritual "organ" into a powerful spiritual muscle. As you exercise it, suffering decreases and self-confidence and happiness increase. The Gap is eventually closed when the well-exercised inner self has become like a guiding compass in your life.

Change How You Interact in Your Suit with the External World

You can put your attention on five practices:

1. Practice acceptance
2. Pause and suspend judgement
3. Practice observing your suit
4. Reframe your thoughts
5. Check your expectations

We have already discussed acceptance in chapter 6, so here I will concentrate on the remaining practices.

Pause and Suspend Judgement

We tend to act without stopping to reflect on what we really want to say or do. It's as if we are on automatic pilot, just saying the first thing that comes to our mind, and reacting based on our initial emotions. Some of the time, this might not seem to matter. But in a situation where something unexpected has happened, or where other people have strong feelings or opinions, our knee-jerk reactions can create problems.

The practice of pausing is valuable because it gives you a chance to observe your own suit's responses and the responses of others in social and work situations. You can use this practice in real-time external events, and you can also use it to resolve past emotional issues. This practice is especially relevant when an external event occurs at home (e.g. your partner comes home after a long day at work and feels tired).

It is also relevant during challenging communications (e.g. you are criticised or verbally attacked by a friend). It is useful during decision making, especially if you are not certain that a decision you are about to make feels right at a gut level.

As you can see from Figure 6, the key to this practice is to pause for a few seconds after an external event occurs. Before you react to the situation, wait two or three seconds. I'm not talking about a long pause that other people will notice. This is a quick and subtle adjustment of perception.

Figure 6. The Practice of Pausing

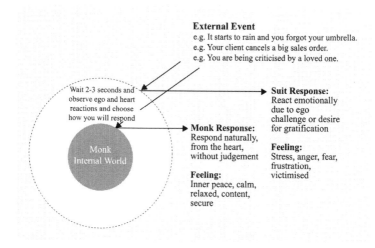

In this time frame, short as it may be, space is created between your suit and your monk, your mind and heart. In this space, you become an observer of your own self. You can observe your thoughts, your viewpoints, your attachment to beliefs you hold, and emotions related to your initial reaction. Also observe the conversation and behaviours of those around you. Be especially careful to note those who seem to be coming from their suit. It is important that you suspend judgement. An observer is a neutral party who observes his or her suit. There is great power in this state of suspended judgement because it keeps you from saying or doing things that can put you on the spot as you consider how best to respond. Don't try to change the situation, but instead accept what is happening without judgement. What already happened cannot be changed, but you can change the way you react or respond to it.

Practice Observing your Suit

Learning to pause and suspend judgement cannot be mastered on one occasion. It takes time and practice. I call this practice *observing your suit*. Like practicing any new skill, in the beginning it might feel odd because you are not used to it but the more you practice, the more easily you will be able to respond to situations and connect with people at heart level.

We all have a social identity that involves adjusting ourselves so we can engage in positive social relations. But the ego can push our social self into a false identity that is not aligned with our true self. This is one of the causes of inner tension. Our mind has to work very hard to keep up what is actually a pretense. If we can observe this happening when we are engaged in it, we have the chance to choose whether and how we rein in the false identity and allow our true self to be expressed in the situation.

As Figure 7 shows, you can choose the pathway of an egoic response or a pathway that will lead to inner peace and to greater connection with others. Of course, you can decide in the moments that follow to remove yourself from the situation. However, simply removing yourself while still mentally resisting or rejecting what has happened does not count as acceptance.

Observing your suit will enable you to see when people are either wrongly putting you down or wrongly putting you on a pedestal. Recently, the organiser of an event at which I was speaking asked me to move the time of my presentation toward the end of the programme because other speakers were being added. She emailed to say it would be better to let the audience warm up first because my part "would be the most brilliant one". Although her intent was to be kind, she could not know whether my presentation would be brilliant nor what the audience would think of me. Her words were just flattery.

After the presentation, a few people expressed their pleasure and that gave me joy. The inner self feels joy when its talents are functioning and flowing in life. The ego, on the other hand, is never too sure about the quality of its talents, and seeks ways to position itself and compensate for any performance shortfalls.

Reframe Your Thoughts

Another practice that you can do to reduce the Gap when you interact with the external world is to reframe your thoughts. Our thoughts have great power as you know from the suffering you experience whenever your mind perceives a problem. Fortunately, that suffering can be eliminated simply by accepting what happened and reframing your so-called "problem". Stop seeing your experience as a problem. When you shift your perception in this way, your suffering is transformed. In the words of the Buddha, "Our life is shaped by our mind; we become what we think. Joy follows a pure thought like a shadow that never leaves".[15]

That sounds simple enough. But how do you do it? Here are some specific steps for reframing your thoughts.

1. First, obvious as it seems, you have to be able to recognise when you are having negative thoughts. These can be thoughts about something in the external world or self-critical thoughts. Often we engage in negative thinking so automatically that we don't realise we are doing it. We're just used to "having problems".

2. To recognise the quality of your thinking, you can apply the

---

15. Eknath Easwaran (Ed.), The Dhammapada, (Tomales, CA: Nilgiri Press, 1993).

practice of pausing, which we discussed in the previous section. When you take a pause, take a barometer reading of your thoughts. One way to do this is to pay attention to key phrases that come up in your mind. Listen to your self-talk, or how you describe things to yourself. For example, you may often use phrases such as "I'm such an idiot" or "I can't stand it when…" or "#$@%&!!" Also pay attention to the tone you use with yourself, and the emotions that accompany your self-talk.

3. Now make an effort to flip your negative thoughts. If you are being self-critical, first accept that you were self-critical and then say something positive to yourself. For example, if you told yourself you were an idiot for forgetting to pay a bill on time, you might accept the fact that you forgot and tell yourself, "I was overworked and I made an honest mistake. I will simply pay the extra fee and make myself a note so I won't do it again". In other words, don't be so hard on yourself. If you are seeing something as a problem, you can reframe it as a challenge instead of a problem.

4. At first when you reframe your thoughts, you may feel that you are being fake with yourself. If you are used to seeing something as a problem, just telling yourself it is not a problem after all may not feel believable. This is where practice comes in. The habit of seeing problems was acquired over years, so it may take a bit of time to alter it. Just keep reframing, and sooner or later your mind will catch up with your good intentions.

Check Your Expectations

It is important to understand the relationship between your expectations and the Gap. Having strong expectations means you project a certain desired outcome. That then starts to become a factor in how you feel. You think, for example, "If I get that promotion, I will be happy; if I don't get it, I will be unhappy". In this way, your expectations of the external world determine your happiness and unhappiness. If your expectation is not met, the Gap increases.

A way of dealing with this is to reduce your expectations. This doesn't mean you do a shoddy job because you expect a poor outcome. No, it means you do the best you can to get that promotion, but you are not attached to the outcome. If you don't get it, you accept that, let it go, and move on.

The same applies in your relationships. Lower your expectations of other people, such as family members, children and friends. If your expectations of others are too high and they don't deliver or perform to meet *your* standards, both of you may feel frustrated. Instead, focus on loving and appreciating your friends and family for who they are, with all their differences. Remember that the joy they bring often outweighs any mistakes they might make.

In addition to checking your expectations about major life events, such as career directions or relationship decisions, you can check expectations on a moment-to-moment basis. For example, suppose you didn't expect much traffic on your drive to work, and suddenly there is a traffic jam. If you go with your immediate feeling and reaction, notice what happens to your Gap. But if you pause and check your expectations, you will realise that traffic is an unpredicatable event. Your best option is to accept the situation. If you're running late, call your co-workers and explain. There is no good reason to let the situation affect your inner state. In fact, most outcomes in the external world are beyond your control anyway, so why become attached to them?

Effectively Manage Your Emotions and Feelings

The second way of closing the GAP is to pay attention to our emotions and feelings. Many of us carry the memory of both positive and negative feelings from when we were a child, teenager, or young adult. These include emotional issues that we have not resolved, such as stress, unhappiness, grief, anger, sorrow, and guilt. If you don't find a way to manage and resolve these emotions, they will continue to create and feed a Gap. Like the practice of reframing thoughts, this is possible to do, though you cannot expect to accomplish it with a snap of your fingers. Here are five practices you can do to get started.

1. Listen to the messenger
2. Deal with negative emotions
3. Resolve inner conflicts
4. Forgive
5. Face your fears

Listen to the Messenger

Emotions are messengers from your body that give you signals of comfort or discomfort. They can help you identify where you need to make changes in your life. For this reason you want to listen to them very carefully. This exercise will help you identify your emotions and help you see how they can benefit you.

For the coming week, three times a day write down the emotions you experience. One time can be about your work. A second time can be about your relationships (e.g. with a partner, friends, or coworkers). The last time can be about yourself. If you are not sure how to identify emotions, see the list in Appendix A.

When you become conscious of your emotions in this way, you have the opportunity to make changes in the environment or within yourself that can greatly reduce your frustration.

Afterwards, reflect on the emotions you wrote down during the week. Ask yourself:

- Why did I feel that way?
- What message is each emotion trying to give me?
- Is there a pattern here?
- Are there any actions I should take?

A variation on this exercise is to focus on recognising and accepting your negative thoughts and feelings about yourself. This isn't an exercise I suggest you practice repeatedly because the point is not to become involved and identified with these negativities. But before you can be free of something you must recognise that you have it. All of us have something about ourselves we don't like or that causes us to feel insecure or even ashamed.

For this exercise, write about something that makes you feel inadequate or unhappy about yourself. For example, it could be the way you look, how you relate to others or how you perform at work. First write about the emotions that arise when you think about this aspect of yourself. Remember, this is only between you and the paper so be as honest as you can.

Then listen for the message. Write about how you can become free of these negativities. When you start you might not know exactly how to go about this. But let the message come through as you write.

Deal with Negative Emotions

When you experience a negative emotion, the first thing is to become aware that you are experiencing a negative emotion. Negative emotions usually originate in the mind. They are based on negative thought patterns. We tend to be over-whelmed by our thought patterns, but if you make the effort to become an observer and be aware of a negative emotion, you can distance yourself from that emotion.

The next step is to identify what made you experience that negative emotion. Pay attention and listen to your inner self. What is your body telling you? What message is given to you through that negative emotion? When you learn more about the negative emotion, your ego has less reason to identify with it.

The final step is to accept that the emotion is one aspect of your experience; it is one of many emotions you will encounter in the natural course of living. By accepting it, you will be able to let it go, as we discussed in the last chapter. Part of letting it go can include getting out of the situation you are in. Sometimes this is the most obvious and practical course of action. If you can't do that, see if you can find a way to be in the situation without experiencing it as negative.

Let me give you an example of how this worked for me. As part of my morning routine, I often used the subway in China to travel to work. It was never a comfortable place for me. At a certain point, I became so frustrated in the subway that I almost burst out in anger. This led me to consider what might be happening. Why the sudden anger? My first thought was that something must be wrong with me because other people seemed perfectly comfortable in the noisy, crowded environment. So I started doing research on the Internet to find out why one person might be sensitive while others were not. When I found Elaine Aron's[16] book about highly sensitive people, I realised I fit her description of a highly sensitive person. With this awareness, I now often choose to avoid visiting very crowded places or places with lots of noise. At other times, when taking the subway is a necessity, I use earplugs and accept the crowded environment for what it is without needing to react in anger.

Resolve Inner Conflicts

It is difficult to hear the messages of your inner monk when your mind and various emotions are constantly engaged in battle. Many of these conflicts have been there practically your entire life, so it may be hard to think you can resolve them now, especially without seeking professional psychological help. But if you are on a journey to close your Gap, this is exactly what you can and must do. Fortunately, techniques are available that can be effective when done on your own.

One practice I recommend is derived from the work of Gestalt therapist Fritz Perls.[17] It is known as the empty chair technique. In this version, you will use three chairs to hold a dialogue between different parts of yourself. You might be tempted to skip the physical chairs since no one is watching you, but don't. Moving from chair to chair is an important way to make this dialogue real and effective. Here I describe how you can use it

---

16. Elaine Aron, The Highly Sensitive Person (New York, Birch Lane, 1998).

17. Fritz Perls, Gestalt Therapy Verbatim, (Boulder, CO: Real People Press, 1969).

for issues involving self-criticism or an unresolved inner conflict.

1. Place three empty chairs in a circle so they face each other. Chair #1 is your inner critic. Chair #2 is your criticised self. Chair #3 is your observer.

2. Focus on your unresolved inner conflict and sit in chair #1. Give a voice to your inner critic and speak to your criticised self (empty chair #2). Say all the negative things you may be feeling (e.g. "You're a failure!" "You never try hard enough". "Everyone hates you".)

3. Now move to chair #2. As your criticised self, this is your chance to respond to your inner critic. Defend yourself (e.g. "When you say that, I feel crushed". "You don't know what I really feel". "I'm not all those ways you say".)

4. Move back and forth between chairs #1 and #2 for as long as you need to complete the dialogue. Notice how you feel in each chair.

5. Take chair #3, the observer. This is the same observer you met in the pause exercise and that you have been practicing with in order to close the Gap while you interact in the external world. Here the observer will serve as moderator between your inner critic and criticised self. Talk to each chair and share what you have observed. For example, you might ask the inner critic, "Do you see how your beliefs create the Gap?" You might tell the criticised self, "I see you are hurting, but the inner critic will become silent and lose his power if you can accept yourself". See if your observer can resolve the inner conflict by talking to both chairs in this manner.

When I first used this exercise, I used only two chairs. I put my inner self in one of them and said, "I'm sorry for not having listened to you for so many years. I'm sorry for neglecting you.

I'm sorry for hurting you. I'm sorry for not trusting you". After I said those things to my inner self, I cried for days. It was a healing experience. I reestablished the connection with my inner monk and my past emotional issues were resolved over time. Similarly, if a loved one has passed away, you can imagine that person sitting in front of you and tell the person whatever you feel like saying.

A client of mine, Sonia, who is a director for a multinational organisation in China also did the empty chair exercise using two chairs. She addressed what she called her "little girl" part, which she went into whenever she felt blamed by others. Sonia said the little girl cried and said to her, "There is a candle inside your heart that represents the hopes and dreams I have pursued for so many years".

Sonia said, "When I was blamed by others, the little girl in me saw a strong wind trying to blow the candle out. She did her best to protect the flame even when I blamed her and called her stupid and foolish. In the end, my blaming her was the strongest wind, and it extinguished the candle. It put her in the dark. I almost cried my heart out because I was the one who hurt her most".

Sonia embraced her little girl and said, "I apologise, I was so wrong. From now on, I will trust you, and believe you. Let's light the candle and make the heart bright, no matter how strong a wind blows, we will be together to protect the candle".

Practice Forgiveness

To bridge the Gap is to heal past emotional issues. Often forgiveness serves as the key to doing this. To connect from the heart with another person, you can write a letter to apologise about something you may have done and to ask for forgiveness. For example, if your frustration leads you to respond to your boss with anger or aloofness, see what happens if you express forgiveness to him or her.

Face Your Fears

When fear controls you, you are stuck; when courage is present, you are ready to close the Gap. A couple of years ago, I became so fed up with all the negativity around me and within myself that I decided to face all my fears one by one. Public speaking, talking to strangers, and trying new things were all challenges to be worked on. Instead of running from these situations, I intentionally scheduled workshops that required me to stand in front of groups of people, sometimes for whole days at a time. Whereas before I avoided opportunities to speak with strangers, I began to embrace those opportunities every chance I could.

These were challenging times for me, and it took two years to experience a shift in how fear controlled me. At the same time, my Gap was gradually closing and my journey became more enjoyable because I was being true to myself. By overcoming these fears I nurtured my heart, which led me closer to my true destination. As a result I became much happier.

Take Time Regularly to Listen to and Nurture your Inner Monk

A final way to bridge the Gap is to nurture yourself by listening to your heart and following your intuition. Once you get in touch with your inner self, you may find yourself torn between your heart and your mind, or your spirit and your ego. This can be very confusing at times, particularly when you need to make decisions. You may want something in your heart, but your mind may hold you back. There are a number of approaches you can use to establish a better connection and communicate with your inner monk.

1. Do some heart work
2. Practice trust
3. Follow your intuition
4. Live in the flow

Do Some Heart Work

By heart work, I mean withdrawing temporarily from the noise of life so you have the space to be still and reflect and to reconnect with your inner self. Some people do this by meditating fifteen or twenty minutes a day.

Meditation helps you still your mind so you naturally return to your inner self. Sitting quietly can be difficult, especially in the beginning but as you practice, it becomes easier. You don't have to sit down to practice meditation. You can withdraw yourself just as effectively while walking, running, or sitting alone on the train. When you cook, you can still your mind by being completely observant of the cooking process: this is meditation. Painting can be meditation. In my case, riding my motorcycle is meditation. As I feel the wind, look at the clouds, feel the sunshine on my skin, my mind becomes calm. The deep connection I experience with myself is beautiful.

The main criterion for heart work to take place is being alone, at least during the initial exercise. As you become more familiar at it, it will become second nature and you can practice it under any circumstance.

This practice is similar to what I described as listening to the messages given by your emotions. In this case, you are listening more deeply and broadly to the messages from your inner monk. In time and with patience, you will be able to pick up messages that have a different sense or resonance than that of your normal mental processes. These messages are rather gentle and so can easily be dismissed, especially if they seem irrational or even a little crazy in their intent.

I encourage you to stay with these messages, and return to them and watch them grow within. They may be indicators of future decisions to be made in your family life or career. They may be prompts toward an activity you did not seriously consider before, such as visiting an art gallery or attending a sports event. Maybe they are prompts to visit someone or to contact a person you don't know well. Don't be fooled if these messages seem to indicate a path of action that offers little or no financial return. As you listen more closely to these messages, your inner self may exude a kind of inner joy that will help keep you on track. As you begin to act on these messages, notice if a new kind of confidence emerges—not one based on external success, but one that reflects the process of becoming a whole person.

Beth tried this exercise after she attended my workshop and wrote an email reporting on her experience. She began by describing what happened at the beginning of her busy week. "On Monday I met an old woman when I walked into the office area. She was cleaning in the miniature garden, and she looked poor and tired. I smiled at her because I wanted to make her feel better. She smiled back immediately, and her eyes were full of warmth and kindness. We watched each other and smiled for a while without talking, and suddenly I felt she looked like my mum. I was very touched".

Beth had such a busy week that she was unable to find time to do any heart work until Friday. She writes: "Finally I got time last night, and as soon as I was alone, the accumulated choking feelings rushed to my heart. I felt a strong flood of emotion break loose, and then it changed to tears. I cried freely because I had the time I needed. All the bad memories reappeared, and my heart felt great pain.

Beth told her inner self, "If a wooden board has been nailed, holes will remain in it even if those nails are removed. Now my heart hurts from all the holes that were put into it by so many nails of criticism, I'm working hard to fill those holes, but some nails still hurt my heart. Please help me to get rid of the pain".

Beth was able to receive a powerful healing message from her inner monk. Her inner monk embraced and comforted her, and said, "You are not alone, I'm with you all the time. And the old woman you met on Monday gave you warmth and kindness. Cry to me whenever you want. You really need to let go of the bad memories and not hide".

109

When, like Beth, you become aware of your emotions and reactions, you open yourself to the connection with your inner monk. Pay attention on a day-to-day basis to what makes you feel comfortable or uncomfortable. Some people resist doing this because they don't want to acknowledge their discomfort, but if you intend to move towards acceptance, you can't cordon off one or another part of yourself. Even in business, emotions are often excluded, so we learn to be rational and lose connection with our emotions and inner self. You have to look at all of it and be completely honest with yourself about what you see and feel.

Develop Trust

The Gap increases when you have difficulty trusting. Because your ego fears being judged by others or you fear something bad will happen, you lose trust. We have already talked about facing your fears. If you've started to practise this, you will have noticed that trust is involved, and that to develop trust, it is essential to surrender.

Surrendering doesn't mean giving in; it means taking a risk and letting go of potentially negative beliefs about what might happen to you. The first time you surrender is likely to be the most difficult, but the more you practise relying on trust, the easier it is. You can surrender to the greater power of the universe and to simply being in the moment, both in relationships and with yourself.

In some cases, following your heart may initially seem to create a worse situation. You may feel that by surrendering or not resisting the other person, you will lose yourself. You want to be trusting but you're afraid of losing yourself. This can lead to a resurgence of fear, especially if you are relying on trust for the first time. In that moment, your mind may take over again but I'm here to tell you to hold on! Give it a bit more of a chance. You may be surprised at how things develop when you are willing to trust.

When I was fired from my job with the freight-forwarding company, it felt like being in free-fall after jumping from an airplane, without a parachute. It was very intense. On the one hand, the sense of freedom and relief was tremendous because no one was telling me what to do. On the other hand, giving up my steady pay check with health insurance, my paid for apartment, my business travel account, company dinners, and much more brought up a lot of deep fear—fear I hadn't yet faced.

In the days that followed, it was hard to think rationally. My security and safety were gone. It seemed as if I had two choices: go back to the corporate environment to retrieve security, or trust that life would guide me in the right direction and everything would work out. The second option felt like the right one, so I chose it. The sense of being in free-fall continued, except now I felt as if the air was carrying me. That gave me a feeling of freedom from everything around me. Taking the initial risk and facing my fears led me to love, to my life purpose, and to writing this book.

Follow Your Intuition

Once you begin to develop trust, the next step is to expand this into every aspect of your life. Following your intuition is one of the biggest challenges you have when transitioning from the external to the internal world. Most people want to be secure and safe and hold onto what they have. Yet holding onto anything external holds you back from being free. What is required is a paradigm shift. Instead of relying on fear and operating out of the mind and intellect, you have to rely on trust, operate from the heart, and follow your intuition.

One of my previous trainers approached me saying that he had an opportunity to work for a company in the suit of director. He would make US$200,000 a year, which my business was unable to pay him. In fact, at that point, my company only paid him a small training fee and no salary because we were too small to pay more.

He faced a tough choice: either stay with me or take the new opportunity. He said he was not passionate about the new opportunity but if he worked there for another ten years, he could retire. That was a strong motivating factor. Even though his intuition knew he was not passionate, his suit told him it was a good opportunity.

After a month of inner conflict over this decision, he came to me and said, "I would like to enjoy the journey of my life, and I believe I can do that best by working with you. Yes we make less money, but it's more enjoyable. For the coming ten years, I want to be free to choose when I wake up, to spend my time teaching instead of attending meetings, and to help people with purpose rather than simply work for money". He said, "Ten years is 3,650 days for me to enjoy all of that".

A very easy method to make the right choices in your life and career and to build self-confidence is to ask yourself at every decision point, "Is this *me*?" Then wait for a few seconds and look deeply within and notice what you feel about the decision. If you feel any hesitation or resistance or slight discomfort in your body, it is a message telling you that it is likely this is not for you.

In this way, your inner monk speaks to you and acts as your trusted advisor. He tells you whether a decision is right for you, or not. It might be right for someone else, but not for you. Chris, one of my coaching clients, carries a small piece of paper in his pocket on which he has written "Is this *me*?" Every time he has to make a decision, he first takes out the paper and asks himself this question. Because he takes the time to get in touch with his inner self, he is able to make the right choice.

Of course, the ego will always keep your mind busy with its own questions. It knows that if it stops being busy you might awaken and render it useless. In fact, there is no true answer to all your mental questions, and there doesn't have to be. The questions from your mind can be answered by facts, but the true questions from the spirit cannot be answered that way.

Once you stop relying on the mind, you will find the answers to your questions within your heart.

Often we already know what our intuition is suggesting, but we don't pay attention to it. Our ego talks us into making decisions that feed it, rather than the true self. For example, leaving a relationship might give you tremendous freedom and relief, yet your ego will fear losing the other person and the affection you're used to receiving. Your intuition says you should leave but because of your fear you don't. In this case, the challenge is to step out of your comfort zone and do what feels right.

Kim, an Australian in her twenties who works for a multinational company in Europe discovered this unexpectedly. She shared a story with me about something that happened to her after participating in a workshop. She was lying in bed at 11 pm one night, when her phone rang. Because she was already in bed, she decided to let it ring, however, she had a strong intuition that she should pick up the phone. She then recalled hearing in the workshop that it is important to follow your intuition. Although she was reluctant to get up, she nevertheless went to the phone and picked it up. Only a few seconds later, the roof of her house above her bed collapsed. She would have been severely injured if she hadn't followed her intuition.

Following your intuition can be difficult because the duality between heart and mind has been with us from an early age. As children, we were taught to place credence on logic and to make decisions based on logic and thought. If a concept cannot be proven by science, our society tends to reject it. For this reason, even if you have experienced extraordinary things beyond what the mind can understand, you probably wrote them off as weird or strange. Especially in the professional world, such things are usually rejected.

Your intuition and internal feelings are the most powerful

guides on your life journey. These feelings already know where they want to go, so you need to learn to listen to them in every situation. Everything is connected in your life, and your feelings will connect you with the things around you. A life lived purely from the perspective of the mind is not very colourful but when you follow your intuition, your internal world can flourish. Many artists and musicians find they do their best work when they are not thinking. This happens because a greater force takes over. Imagine what the world would be like if everyone stopped acting from their thoughts and started following their intuition and creativity.

How can you make this 180 degree shift from thoughts to feelings? If your mind has been busy and in control for many years, your inner monk may be afraid to come out. Talking to yourself helps to connect with him. For example, you may say, "I am sorry I have neglected you for so long. It is safe to come forward. I will be there for you and protect you. Please, I need your help".

David's friend was on subway line number 10 in Shanghai when suddenly he got the intuition that he had to get off the train when the doors opened. This was before his intended destination. One stop later he felt the same urge to get off the subway, and he couldn't explain it. One more stop and the feeling became immense. He said to himself, "It doesn't make sense to get off, I haven't arrived yet". So he didn't. The doors closed. What happened next was devastating. The train crashed full speed into another train that was standing still. David's friend ended up in hospital with a broken arm and leg.

Rationally you won't always be able to understand why you should do something. But it can be a matter of life and death. For this reason, you need to learn how to listen to your inner monk.

It is often said that you should think first and then act. However, when faced with a challenge, the ideal response—provided you're in touch with your heart—is to act first and then think. Spontaneous action flows from the heart, which knows what is right and best. If you allow yourself to respond spontaneously and act straight from your heart, you will be following your intuition. If you act using your mind and thinking first, the response becomes calculated and you will end up weighing the pros and cons and deciding what you think is best for you, even if it is not what feels right. So always follow the first thing that comes to you. If your first feeling is no, then say no; if it is yes, say yes. Let your decision be natural.

Living in the Flow

Flow is one of the most important principles in the universe. In chapter 3, I mentioned the Taoist concept of *tao*, which refers to the flow of the universe and which keeps everything balanced and in harmony. In this flow, there are no challenges. Everything is taken care of.

Perhaps you have had the experience of flow when being so involved in a work project that you end up losing all sense of time. Time as we know it no longer seems to exist as we become fully engrossed in the task at hand. We experience flow in our day-to-day lives when we surrender and allow our lives to unfold moment by moment. This flow is a constant surrendering, trusting, following of intuition, and allowing things to happen.

I always used to plan activities well in advance. The ideas that came to me were good, and the prospect of doing them was very exciting. However, often when the day came to implement a plan, my mood had changed. In that moment, entirely differ-ent seemed more appealing. As a creature of habit, my tendency was to stick to the plan simply because it was my plan. However, as time went by, this worked less and less well. I found that going with the flow worked better and gave me a new and delightful way of experiencing life. Sometimes this

115

flow brings me to a restaurant with a discount or to a hidden place in the city, revealing a shop that has just what I needed at that moment.

How do you discover your flow? Flow cannot be discovered; it is simply a way of living. Bankei Yotaku, a Zen Buddhist master, once said, "You know only one miracle—to allow nature to have its own course. You don't interfere". This is really very simple, straightforward guidance. In other words, don't try to force the natural rhythm of life. When something happens, act spontaneously. Don't try to change something external just because someone says you should or because it is taught in books or has been scientifically proven. Everything will change automatically if you allow it to happen.

Don't worry about whether or not it's the right thing to do, just go with your flow. If there is a beggar on the street and you feel like giving something to him, just give. If you start looking around first to see whether someone might be watching you, you are not being authentic. Life works in such a way that when you are open to accepting things in life and allowing them to happen, the right people and situations come into your life. Love naturally and powerfully flows within your being and you know in your heart that you are completely open and free. This is the true unchangeable happiness.

Try this: Next weekend, when you go out of your house, simply allow things to happen. Don't think too much, instead act spontaneously based on your feelings. See where the flow takes you. However, be aware that the real world as we know it (businesses, the media, our social system and so on) moves faster than the natural flow of life, and we are therefore in danger of falling into the wrong current.

Let me explain by using a Taoist story. An old man fell into a river that was upstream from a mighty waterfall. He got swept away, but fortunately managed to make it over the falls without getting hurt. As he stepped out of the river below, people asked him how he survived. "I didn't think about it", he said. "I let myself be shaped by the water; I just went with its flow and didn't try to shape the water",

Living in the flow opens us up to new levels of creativity. My experience of the flow gave me great insights on the content of the book you now hold in your hands. When you go with the flow, you experience everything in life just as it is. So stop trying so hard and just let go.

Mind the Gap

The good news is that once you start to listen to your inner monk, life can only get better. The more your spirit expands, the more you are courageous and follow your heart and the less your ego will have grounds to resist.

For me, the paradoxical image of a suited monk captures the essence of what it means to close or bridge the Gap. As a suited monk, you are in touch with and flow naturally between the external and internal worlds—wearing the suit of the business world or your job, yet receiving guidance from your inner world. For example, you can wear a tough-looking police uniform because that is required by your job and at the same time remain in touch with your heart because you want to help people. You can wear the apron of a bread baker and enjoy baking because it is your purpose to make bread for people and you enjoy doing so. In the suit of a CEO, you can build a business to serve the community through your inner monk. This is the essence of bridging the Gap. Being a suited monk might sound like a tough juggling act if you haven't experienced it before but once you bridge the Gap, you will find it becomes effortless.

As you close the Gap and the attachment to your suit dissolves, you will literally wake up. In Buddhism, this is called *enlightenment*, or the end of suffering. When you awaken, all your suffering, unhappiness, and negative emotions simply disappear. Often this is a gradual process that can sneak up on you before you realise what has happened. Once you have awoken, you begin to live from the heart at every moment. You are able to give freely and to receive and accept changes easily; in life, in your relationships, and at work. There is nothing for you to defend against and so you live at ease and at peace with yourself. You can compare an awakening to naturally waking up in the morning without an alarm: it just happens, there's nothing you must do, you just wake up. I will discuss this more fully in the next chapter.

Figure 7. Suit and Monk are in Alignment

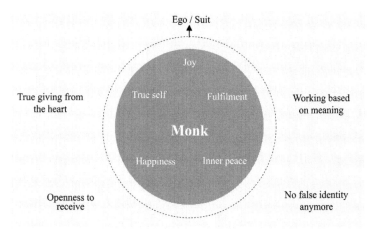

In some London Underground stations, passengers have to cross a wide gap to step onto the train. For their safety, the public address systems announce, "Mind the Gap!" In your future life and career, please *Mind the Gap*.

Chapter 8

Discovering Your Inner World

8.Discovering Your Inner World

As you close the Gap, your inner monk wakes up and your own potential begins to unfold. This brings into alignment your inner passion, highest talents, life purpose, and the expression thereof in the external world. Your life journey involves discovering who you are, what you are born to do; it involves following your heart and finding your purpose and aligning this purpose with the external world.

The inner world is rich in so many ways. When I first arrived in Shanghai, I lived in a cheap service apartment which was a huge change from the lifestyle I previously enjoyed. I didn't want my partner to suffer as a result of my decision to pursue a more meaningful career, so I told her she could choose any apartment she wanted and I would make sure we could pay for it. She said this was impossible because she wanted to live in a nice place, minimum US$1,500 per month and we clearly didn't have the money. The day before we went in search of an apartment, I asked the universe to help us find the place we wanted for only US$900. I held the image of a nice apartment for that price in my head and in my mind I asked, "Please help us find a nice but affordable place". I directed these words to the universe, whilst also directing them to my inner self, knowing that they were intimately connected. You could say the words came from my inner self, were directed to my inner self, and also answered by my inner self. The next day, to my surprise we found exactly the place we wanted, for exactly US$900, in fact, it was the best apartment we had ever had!

When you are in touch with your inner world, you always know the right way to respond because your heart is aware of the energy in the world around you. It is also in tune with the vast energy of the universe. Truly speaking, a person who can't trust his or her own heart will end up like dry leaves on a windy autumn day.

121

The Internal Journey

The internal journey was described by mythologist Joseph Campbell [18] as a "hero's journey" in his timeless model for personal change. However, the internal journey is not only for mythical heroes and storybook fantasies. It is a way of living that leads to a consistent feeling of joy, happiness, and inner peace. Every human being has the right to peace and contentment.

Living with heightened awareness of yourself and the world around you is extremely powerful. With a more finely tuned level of clarity, you can see where your true path lies and thus reap the benefits of your maximum personal potential in life and at work.

The main challenge you face is that the mind easily adapts to its external surroundings; it likes to settle into its comfort zone and create a structure that is familiar and predictable. When you reach a new level of clarity or a point of great joy, it's tempting to think, "This is it. I've finally arrived". You try to maintain this level of satisfaction by doing the same thing again and again, but much to the surprise of your mind, it no longer works. Why is this? The law of diminishing marginal returns exerts itself, and the same circumstances do not give you an equal degree of satisfaction the second, third, or fourth time around.

Some people consciously search for their inner world. In the same way they push themselves within their career, they also push themselves to achieve their highest potential. Unfortunately, after many attempts, they still haven't found what they were seeking. The reason is that your inner self can't be "found". It is impossible to find because you already *are* your inner self: it is not something that has actually ever been "lost". Once you stop searching and begin to observe yourself, what

18. Joseph Campbell, The Hero with a Thousand Faces (New York: Pantheon, 1949).

you were searching for will automatically reveal itself. This happens when you are able to bridge the Gap. When the Gap is bridged, it is as if you can see, feel and observe your spirit beyond the ego. Nothing needs to be done, nothing has to happen, and nothing has to change—except a shift in focus from your external to your internal world (Figure 4).

In the *Tao Te Ching*, poet Lao Tzu expressed this beautifully:

> If you want to become full,
> let yourself be empty.
> If you want to be reborn,
> let yourself die.
> If you want to be given everything,
> give everything up. [19]

Like the image of the suited monk, the words in this poem are paradoxical. Letting yourself be empty means going beyond the ego and operating from your heart, which is both empty and completely full. When you let yourself die, you awake, as the dissolving of the ego leads to the rebirth of the spirit. Paradoxically, by giving up everything—your feeling of attachment to things, your egoic identity, your fears—you make it possible to wake up and return to the spirit, which gives you everything you ever needed.

Discovering your internal world takes courage. You must believe and trust in yourself and in life; surrender and follow your intuition and inner journey; accept things as they are and be willing to let go of old thoughts, beliefs, negative emotions and attachments that are no longer useful along your journey. Initially, you may experience temporary discomfort and unease, for example, unsettling emotions from past experiences or you may face uncertainty and new challenges. However, the more you become aware of your inner being, the clearer and easier your path will become. You can compare this journey to a

---

19. Lao Tzu, Stephen Mitchell, trans., Tao Te Ching (New York: Harper Perennial, 1991), 22.

well with a special water pump that only works in one direction. Once it's been opened, it can't be closed. The further you raise the handle, the more water will flow out. In a similar way, once your journey has begun, the process is naturally revealed. All you need to do is follow the flow; it isn't necessary to know where it will end.

One of my coaching clients shared the story of her inner journey with me. Jiao was working in a well-paying job in her hometown in China, but her heart was telling her to go to South China to work. Her husband said it would be better if she stayed and worked at home because she already had a good job and also had a one-year-old child. However, she felt a strong inner pull so despite opposition from her parents, whose cultural view was that family is one of the most important elements in a person's life, she decided to go anyway.

Jiao went to South China with a budget of US$250 for two months. She paid US$150 in rent and had US$100 left for transportation, food, and to find a job. As the end of the second month approached, still without a job, she had to reduce her food intake from three meals a day to two. Because she only had US$10 left, she walked rather than taking public transportation. Her husband continuously asked her to come home.

Finally, Jiao landed a job as the marketing manager of a multinational company. Soon after, her husband followed her and also got a job there. Jiao loves her job and said she would make the same decision again. Her journey led her to discover her life's purpose. She said, "My journey was never about making money. It was about searching for something I love to do and about following my heart. It's been hard, but at least I am enjoying my journey!"

As Jiao's story shows, walking the journey is about making choices that allow you to remain true to yourself, even though you may have to make sacrifices as you let go of the old and open yourself to new possibilities and directions. In these moments, have the courage to trust in yourself and to trust in life.

It is within that space of trust that you will find freedom in your life.

Are you on the internal journey?

Whatever job you may have, you can walk the internal journey. In fact, you may be walking it now without even realising.

Ask yourself:

- Am I working mainly for money or to fulfill my purpose in life?
- Am I working to receive or working to give?
- Do I love what I do?

The answers to these questions reveal the difference between being on the external and being on the internal journey. For example, if you are working merely to receive money, your experience of life will be very different than if you are working first and foremost to do what you love. If you don't love what you do, life will appear challenging and it is because you are working against your inner self that this resistance arises.

You might think that a woman whose job is cleaning the floor in a restaurant could never truly enjoy her work, after all, who wants to clean? But I have met such people and asked them what they enjoy about their work. One person said, "For me, this is art". Hearing this, I knew she was on the internal journey. There was no resistance toward the job she was doing; rather, she saw it as an expression of her inner self. She was like a suited monk, fulfilling what she knew to be her purpose in life, regardless of how it might have appeared to anyone observing.

I discuss finding your purpose in detail in chapter 10. For now, it's enough to understand that you find your purpose through self-awareness because that is the essence of who you are. You are not your mind, you are your heart. Everyone is born with a purpose. Only by knowing your true purpose and following your intuition will you be able to fully enjoy what life has to offer. It's like walking in a forest. You can either choose a path which others are walking and you know to be safe and secure, or you can choose the path to which you feel most called, whether it feels safe and secure or not, This path may be the same that others are walking or it may be one that no one has walked before. Either way, if you follow your inner calling, you will walk the journey the universe has laid out for you and be surprised to discover the true wisdom and joy that life has to offer.

Become more Conscious and Aware

When he was in his fifties, Michael Gates Gill had everything he wanted: a high-paying job, a wonderful home life, and good health. But then he lost it all. He was fired, his wife left him, and he was diagnosed with a slow-growing brain tumor. One day as he sat in Starbucks, nursing a latté he could barely afford, the store manager approached and offered him a job. The offer was made half in jest, but almost before he knew what was happening, Michael found himself in a Starbucks uniform serving coffee. Suddenly, he was forced to become conscious and aware in ways he had never been before. It didn't matter that his younger coworkers lacked his level of education and work experience; they had lots to teach him about how to live life. He discovered that he derived great joy from simply serving people and brightening up their day with a cup of coffee. He ended up writing a bestseller about his transformation into a happier, humbler, and more aware person.

Life is not about how much money you make, but about how you can express yourself in doing what you love. This has nothing to do with how big your mansion might be; it is about how you feel within and how you serve others in the work you do. Often a wake-up call stimulates that awareness. It may seem to happen by accident, but such a wake-up call usually happens for a reason. It helps you gain greater awareness of yourself and your life, and affords you an opportunity to make changes and grow.

Awareness can be understood as the direct perception of reality without the intervening filter of concepts and ideas. It is the key to self-discovery—a key that is uniquely yours because it can only unlock your inner world, no one else's. Being aware is not limited by your preconceptions, it is fresh and new in every moment. Greater awareness will make it easier for you to find your path in life.

When I speak of being more *conscious,* I am referring to the constant state of awareness in which we are open to receiving signs and messages from the environment around us and from our life circumstances. Our thoughts take on less importance. Instead of analysing, judging, and interpreting everything intellectually, we listen, observe patiently, and simply absorb what is, without labelling the experience. Of course thoughts may be present, coming and going within the realm of the mind, but when we listen to the heart and remain aware, we don't have to engage and become involved in those thoughts; they don't determine our experience of reality.

Awareness brings meaning to your experience. It stimulates learning and questioning, such as asking yourself why you are the way you are, and why things happen or don't happen in your life. Although the goal is not to find a fixed reason for everything, enhanced awareness will give you the ability to make better decisions and to live in a way that aligns your actions with your true desires. You can each reach your destination on the journey by practising awareness in your day-to-day life. By being more aware, you open yourself up to receive whatever gifts life has to offer you—from the most mundane to the most sublime. For this to be attained, you must step outside your comfort zone and journey to the very core of your being.

Some of us live and work unconsciously. We go about our day on automatic pilot. Our job exists only to pay bills. We get up in the morning, get dressed, go to the office, come home, eat dinner, and then go to sleep. It's as if we are hypnotised; as if the external world is the master and we are its slaves. We wear the clothes other people tell us to wear, eat the food others say is popular, and even think thoughts we feel will please others.

When we allow ourselves to be swayed by external influences, it's difficult to remember where we truly belong and who we truly are. Being unaware results in the ignorance of our true self. It also opens us up to unwanted and undesirable external input. Our subconscious mind can be influenced in many ways. For example, we are constantly manipulated by television commercials that lead us to believe we need a particular product to feel happy. The information may bypass our conscious mind and go straight to our subconscious mind. The next thing we know, we are acting on the impulse. Instead, transformation of unaware living into aware living is what is needed in the world today. When we live with full awareness, it is easy to know if we are on the right path. As aware beings, we are naturally in touch with our intuition and true inner feelings. If something happens that makes you uncomfortable, you might ask yourself, "What is this uncomfortable feeling trying to tell me?" If you simply heed the feeling's message and recognise what it is that you need to solve or change, you will stay on the right path.

Practise Awareness

I am not talking about anything complicated. To begin practising awareness, all you need to do is sit down with a book and a cup of coffee or tea. Become aware of your body: feel your feet, your legs, and your hands touching the book. Take a sip of your tea or coffee and notice the feel of the cup, the taste of the drink. Become aware of your surroundings: the furniture, the floor, the light from the windows. When you consciously observe in this way, there is no room for thought. There is no need for interpretation, just observation. Develop the ability to be aware of your context, beyond any words you might use to define it. Try it.

For example, practise awareness by looking at a flower next to you. Notice that as soon as a thought comes in to your head, you lose full awareness of that flower. You can't be fully aware of the flower and think at the same time. It's a subtle distinction, but it makes all the difference between being aware and not being aware.

Of course, I'm not suggesting you try to live without thoughts; that would be highly impractical. But if you expand your awareness, you will be more able to simply enjoy the present moment and discover how your journey is unfolding.

You have a fresh opportunity at every moment of the day in your work and in your life to become more aware. You can eat with or without awareness, you can walk with or without awareness, you can work with or without awareness. When you work with awareness, you are operating from your true self, beyond the mind. You are being an observer of your own self and others, without judging them.

In sum, the outcome of practising awareness is rich:

- You will better understand your own emotions; thoughts; and view of yourself, others, and the world.
- You will be able to suspend judgement about people and life circumstances.
- You will be free from stress, inner tension, and personal conflict.
- You will notice more from an observer's point of view rather than from being caught up in the entanglements of life.
- You will engage in more self-reflection. Awareness allows you to turn off your automatic pilot and ask more meaningful questions; for example, "Why do I do what I do?" "What could I do differently?" "How can I make my life more meaningful?"
- You will make better decisions and find better solutions for yourself, your career, and your relationships.

Raise Your Awareness

Pause for a moment and take stock of your awareness. How strong is it? Ask yourself: How often do I choose to take a different route to work? How aware am I while at work? How often do I think about my purpose in life? Perhaps these three questions have different degrees of importance, but all reflect a level of awareness. At the lowest level, it's as though your external life is leading you around on a chain. At a higher level, your inner self takes the lead and your life is guided by intuition and inner wisdom. Our predominant level is determined by training and habit, much like working out at the gym: it only takes a few weeks or so to get out of shape. You can think of awareness as a muscle that needs to be exercised regularly to function at its highest level.

Awareness is like water: pure and clear. When you live in the external world, your awareness can become muddy and stagnant. It can be tainted by all the negative thoughts and impressions that fill your mind and cloud your heart. Only if you filter out that mud by practising awareness can the water become pure and clear again.

Imagine you are an Olympic athlete who aspires to win the gold medal. Your coach acts as a mirror, giving you feedback on your form, method, and habits. To become a medal-winning athlete, you need to remain highly conscious in all areas of your life. Slipping in your diet or exercise regime only a little will affect your performance. Living consciously is like being an athlete in training: it's an ongoing growing process. It's not about reaching some kind of end level; rather, it is the ability to continuously examine your beliefs and behaviours so you can gain a clear perception of your present state, observe it, learn about it, make changes accordingly, and grow.

When you raise your awareness and learn to live more consciously, you come to view life from a greater perspective. It's like turning on the lights one by one in a dark room. Each light you turn on allows you to see more of the room. Instead of randomly stumbling around in the darkness, you're able to see what is in the room and whether you're walking on the right path. In fact, as soon as the first light has been switched on, no matter how dim it may initially be, you are no longer in the dark.

Learning through Awareness

You've probably heard the phrase "knowledge is power". In the external world, the accumulation of intellectual knowledge is essential. We only need to be able to count, read, and write to function in the working world, and yet we take it one step further. Our identity becomes attached to our achievements: if we get good grades at school, we are praised and feel worthy; if we get low grades, we feel unworthy. We identify with our achievements and wear our degrees like a badge. The more knowledge we acquire, the more important we feel.

Of course, good grades and a high IQ can help you achieve external success, however, this type of knowledge won't help you find meaning, purpose, or your inner self. In the internal world, the acquisition of knowledge in itself has no meaning. Accumulating knowledge doesn't necessarily make you wiser, happier, or more fulfilled. If you want to progress on the internal journey, instead of more knowledge, you need greater awareness. You need to learn through awareness and through your own direct experience.

Unfortunately, many years at school do little to put us in touch with our true inner being. In fact, some people are in touch with their true being as young children and actually lose that awareness as they come under the influence of teachers and peers at school. In many ways, our education steers us away from awareness and teaches us to depend on mental knowledge. As a result, after university we enter the external world ready to become successful on the external journey, but not prepared to use the wisdom of our heart.

If you are somebody who doesn't learn well through traditional means of academia, that's not a problem, your purpose may lie in something more creative or practical, like music or art. What I am suggesting is that you be willing to let that which is unknown into your life. For example, consider how you approach this book. If you simply use it to gain more intellectual knowledge such as memorising unfamiliar terms and their order in the model, you won't truly understand what I am saying or gain any lasting value. On the other hand, if you use it as a tool to learn through awareness, you will observe your inner experience as you read and pay attention to how what I am saying might apply in your life.

Cultivate Happiness

As you become more conscious and aware, you will also find it easier to cultivate happiness. This is because your awareness is no longer focused exclusively on what you can obtain in the external world and so you are no longer driven by external wants and needs.

I was recently asked if someone who wants and needs nothing is really happier than someone who has everything. People who look only to the external world for satisfaction invariably want more and more. Such people may become billionaires, but unless they feel connected with their internal world, they are unlikely to feel truly satisfied, happy, or at peace. At the same time, those who have nothing in the external world often crave the success and money they don't have so they too lack happiness. But a third group—those who want and need nothing—experience no obstacles to happiness. It doesn't matter whether such a person is rich or poor; if he or she is rich within, the person will be happy.

Nonattachment and Happiness

Consider the following questions. What is the difference between:

- A rich person who is happy and a rich person who is unhappy?
- A poor person who is happy and a poor person who is unhappy?
- A person who is seriously ill but happy, and a person who is seriously ill and unhappy?

The only difference is whether they are attached to what they have or don't have. For example, if a rich person doesn't need wealth to be happy, he or she isn't attached to it and will remain happy even if it is gone. These people's happiness is dependent on their internal state of being; their own nature. They are not reliant on external circumstances. On the other hand, if a rich person needs wealth to be happy, his or her happiness depends on that wealth. We can say such rich people are attached to their wealth.

The same applies to poor people who are unhappy. For example, if a poor person is attached to a blanket considering it as "mine", and the blanket is then lost, he will feel unhappy. However, a poor person who is not attached to the blanket but uses it only to sleep under will still be happy if the blanket is taken away. Yes, he may be cold and uncomfortable, but that does not affect his lasting state of inner happiness. The blanket itself is not part of who he considers himself to be and so this person trusts that if the blanket has been taken away, there is a reason for it and the universe will help, for example, by providing a bigger blanket, the money to buy another one or some other form of support. Similarly, a sick person who is attached to their illness will become a victim to it making them unhappy. On the other hand, a sick person who has accepted their illness is no longer identified with it and will learn to accept and live with whatever condition their body may undergo. Their happiness depends on their inner being, not the sickness.

What does this mean for you? It means that if you want to find happiness, you can't depend on what you have or don't have at any given point in time. What you have now may be gone tomorrow, and vice versa. For this reason, the best strategy when it comes to your wants and needs is to cultivate nonattachment.

Nonattachment doesn't mean giving up all the things you have and enjoy. It doesn't mean taking a vow of poverty or reassigning yourself to a life of austerity. Some people believe that to live a spiritual life you have to give everything up; this is not true. It's not that because Buddha did it, you should do so too. Buddha's journey was his, your journey is yours. Nonattachment simply means you do not feel possessive or identified over an aspect of your life. You can still be who you are, regardless of what you have or don't have. For example, you can work for a company while not being attached to your position or what you receive in return for the work you do. You can simply enjoy fulfilling your purpose. This is the secret to lasting happiness.

True Happiness Is Lasting

Some researchers have identified a genetic set point for happiness, which implies that most people are not likely to be constantly happy. If this is true, I would have to ask, "Then what am I experiencing? Why do I feel happy every day?" Even when I need to cry or when I feel sad or I am having a difficult time, I am still happy.

This is something the mind cannot easily understand. How could you be happy and unhappy at the same time? This can happen only if you are in touch with your inner monk. When you are connected with your inner self, all negative emotions appear to be on the surface of your being. You don't need to rid yourself of negative emotions to feel lasting happiness. The inner monk is who you really are, everything else comes and goes like a passing show.

If people everywhere are seeking this kind of happiness, how come so few are truly happy in their private life and at work? Often they are busy smiling and pretending to be happy. They become preoccupied looking at others they believe to be happy and feel bad that they aren't as happy as they think those people are. In essence, they are so caught up in the external world that they have little chance of finding lasting happiness. But living in a constant state of happiness is achievable. When your happiness is not dependent on the external world but rather on your internal world, you can achieve a state of constant happiness.

Happiness Is a Choice You Make

Happiness is a choice you make moment to moment. Achieving that state is part of the journey; it is a process. It can't be learned by reading a few books or listening to audio tapes. Nor can happiness be achieved by effort or by reminding yourself to be happy. If you have to set reminders for yourself every morning so you appreciate what you have, then happiness will disappear as soon as you stop putting in the effort to achieve it. Rather, happiness is a state of being, an experience that just happens and is constant. You can cultivate happiness by becoming more aware of your feelings. If you feel unhappy, ask yourself, "Is my unhappiness related to an event in the external world?"

You may think that you won't be able to live in total bliss unless your mind has become free of all thoughts. This is not my experience. Even though I feel happy deep within, I still have thoughts going in my mind. I had to learn to accept and embrace my thoughts without being attached to them. As I walked my journey and discovered my purpose, my thoughts automatically became fewer because I had less cause for worry and less reason to think about doing something different in life.

Traditional mediation is not required to achieve a state of happiness. Simply by following your heart and purpose in life, you can experience it. Happiness doesn't depend on your position or power; it depends on your inner monk. A CEO, for example, is not going to be happier than a manager or a policeman. It doesn't work that way. All you need to do is live the life that is meant for you and experience happiness along the way.

As you can see from the Life Journey Model, it is only when you handle your challenges with acceptance and surrender and follow your intuition that you experience true happiness. In this way, there is less resistance, less pain and less suffering because your Gap is closing. When you do what you love and work in a state of flow and joy, you are overcome by feelings of freedom and happiness. When the ego becomes smaller, inner happiness has a chance to flourish. This is the only route to true happiness.

Past, Present, and Future

A story published in the 1990s and made famous on the Internet since then, tells of a New York taxi driver who picks up an elderly woman with a suitcase. When she asks the driver to take a long route to her destination, he is at first reluctant. But when he learns she has only a short time to live and is on her way to a hospice, he gladly spends the rest of the night giving her a final tour of the city. When they finally arrive, he won't take payment from her and she thanks him by saying, "You gave an old woman a little moment of joy." The driver concludes,[20]"For the remainder of that day, I could hardly talk. What if that woman had gotten a driver who had been angry or abusive or impatient to end his shift? What if I had refused to take the run or had honked once, then driven away?.... How many other moments like that had I missed or failed to grasp? We are so conditioned to think that our lives revolve around great moments. But great moments often catch us unawares."

The taxi driver was there for the elderly woman for the sake of love and kindness, not for money. His was a service role concerned with helping others on their journey. His story reso-nated with me because it illustrates one important quality of the inner world: it is not controlled by time. When you walk the inner journey, you do so in the present moment. All great moments are experienced in the present. Happiness doesn't exist in some distant future and it can't be retrieved from the distant past, only the beauty of the present moment can bring us true fulfillment.

When we focus on the external world, everything revolves around the past and the future; however, when we live in the internal world there is only the present moment. Perhaps you've heard the phrases "be fully present" and "the present is a gift", or heard it said that someone has a "nice presence". But what does this actually mean and why should you want to be more present? To be present means to be fully aware and conscious of yourself and the world around you at any given moment and to appreciate what it has to offer.

20. Kent Nerburn, Make Me an Instrument of Your Peace (New York: HarperCollins, 1999).

Although it may seem like a simple concept, living in the present is a lot more challenging than it sounds, especially in today's fast-paced world. We have so many thoughts pulling our attention in different directions—often to a place other than the here and now, like the taxi driver who could have thought instead about how to make more money in shorter time. The effect of these external stresses is that we don't experience the present moment in its fullest. We lose out on enjoying the moment and miss the messages that may come to us from the circumstances in our lives and from the greater universe. The present moment is reduced to a means to an end; we squander it away by continually delving into thoughts about the past or future. Ultimately, the reason the present is so important is simply because it is the only thing we have. The Buddha said, "Do not dwell in the past, do not dream of the future—concentrate the mind on the present moment".

The past in the external world consists of memories and experiences. These can be either good or bad, depending on your interpretation at the time. For example, if in the past you were told you were an average basketball player, you will carry that memory with you today. If someone said you were a good writer, you will think of yourself as a good writer. This is how identities are formed. Our past in the external world is a reference and a reality we believe to be true. All too often, our decisions about the future are based on our memories and beliefs from the past.

A man who participated in one of my workshops felt stuck in his life because he had formed an image of himself as not good enough. As we dug deeper, he discovered this belief came from his childhood when his father used to call him lazy. Laziness became part of his identity and it held him back. In the workshop, he was able to release this old belief and make room for a new reality in the present.

Have you ever really looked forward to something? For example, perhaps you thought "In three months I'm going to lie on the beach and relax, drink cocktails, have nice meals, enjoy the sunshine and finally find a sense of peace with nothing to think or worry about. But what happened when you finally lay down on the beach? I bet you found yourself thinking about work or other aspects of your life. Somehow we are never able to fully enjoy this present moment.

Our future in the external world is a mental projection of our goals. Our desire for a better life drives us forward. You tell yourself, for example, that you'll be happier in the future, that you'll have a better job, home, or relationship. You plan, plot, and strategise but unfortunately you don't find the inner peace and contentment you crave. You focus on the possibility of future calamities and continue to obsess about "what if": what if you lose your job, suffer an illness, or experience a natural disaster?

Does this mean you don't have valuable past experiences or shouldn't plan for the future? I'm not saying that. You did experience things before, but they were in your present moment then, not in your present moment now. Having goals can be good if you enjoy the flow of working toward your future. However, it is important to recognise that your future goals, purpose, and mission are the outcome of your actions in the present. Moreover, your life journey will naturally unfold regardless of what you do to try and shape it. Life itself will take you there without you having to focus on it.

For example, a friend of mine who is an executive coach told me the story of Ben, a senior executive at a global property developer. With an ever-growing workload, communications across different time zones, and new deals constantly coming into play, he felt increasingly pinched for time. Any downtime he tried to set aside was chewed up by work demands. He kept breaking commitments to his wife, his children, and himself. Ben was left feeling out of control, but what was probably more damaging, was that his world no longer had value.

Unfortunately, a so-called crisis sometimes needs to accumulate in size before for people will respond to it. In Ben's case, his marriage was suffering and that forced him to pay attention. He sought help through coaching and became aware that the work life balance game he was playing was set up for failure because it was based on the linear dimension of time. So he worked with his coach to shift his mindset from "making time" to "making a difference".

Ben identified the most important things in his life. At the top of the list were his relationships with his wife and children. He also identified outcomes he was committed to achieving in those relationships, and instead of trying to fit them into scarce time slots, he looked at how he could set up his life so it produced the outcomes he wanted in those relationships. This change in awareness blew everything open for him. Life became about quality and precious moments together. Priorities shifted and he became an incredibly happier person. This new way of thinking did not just affect his family life, but also went on to have an impact on his work, hobbies, fitness, and beyond.

Have you noticed that often when you go away on vacation, you come back with an understanding about what needs to change in your life? If this happens to you, it is probably because you took the time to be with yourself, without too much thinking. When we are focused in the present moment, inner answers can rise to the surface. Often when we go back to our office, we quickly refocus on the external world and our spirit recedes once again. Many people postpone happiness or what they truly want because they think they have something important to do first. For example, they have to get a promotion, make more money or find the right partner as only then will they be able to change. They put off their happiness in the meantime but the change never comes; happiness remains a future dream. Don't postpone your happiness; it will never happen in the future. Living in the present means enjoying the process of what you are doing. It means practising being aware of yourself and the activities in which you are involved, as I mentioned earlier.

Let me give you another example. When was the last time you tasted what you ate? This may seem an easy question to answer, but I mean *really* tasted? Often you eat only because it is necessary. You know what you are eating, but you fail to actually taste the food. To come into the present and really taste your food, focus your awareness on the food in your mouth and allow yourself to take in the taste as if it were the first time you were experiencing it. After swallowing, wait three seconds before taking another bite. Don't talk; just experience. Try this and see if you don't derive more enjoyment from the food you eat; see if you don't start to notice subtle tastes that previously eluded you.

When one of my friends, Barry, a European manager, was fourteen-years-old, his father lost his business. For eight years, the family was reduced to living in a garage. One Christmas Eve, as they were sitting around an old fireplace in the garage trying to keep warm, Barry's father opened up a bottle of wine. He said, "This is the best wine I could afford, let's enjoy it and celebrate our being here together!" Barry said that moment was an eye opening for him. He became aware of the joy that can be found in the moment, even in the smallest of things. What he might possess in the future was unimportant. He said, "These days I have everything I need, but I still try to appreciate the small things and the present moment as much as I can because it's those moments that make a difference."

I encourage you to find ways to practise becoming more aware of the present moment. See what works for you, whether it is breathing, eating, meditation, or being present in another form you can think of. One practice I often use when I walk outside my home is to feel whatever touches my skin without naming it or putting a label on it. If it is cold, I accept the cold and let it be; I stay present to the cold and feel it on my skin. If it is the sun on my skin, I feel the energy from the sunlight and enjoy the sense of feeling and just being. I often drive my motorcycle around nature and on empty roads to enjoy the experience of both the external world, in this case the motorcycle, and the internal world, the wind, the sun, the hot or the cold on the skin. The longer you stay in the present, the less fear you will have and the greater the chance your spirit and intuition will flourish.

Awakening

The internal journey culminates in awakening. When we awaken, our internal world expands to its full potential and our existence is no longer determined by the external world. What we considered to be real in the external world sometimes takes on a surreal quality.

Once during an evening gathering, someone asked who I was. I said, "I am nobody". Immediately people started to say, "No, Raf, you are somebody. You shouldn't say that about yourself". However, when we awaken, we realise that we are nobody; we literally are *no body*. Our identification with the bodily form is gone and we realise we are not the identity we thought we were. We realise we are the spirit in the body, not the body itself.

Our identification with our suit also disappears. We are left with pure emptiness. This emptiness is our highest state of fulfillment; it is our highest, truest form. We are at one with our inner monk and know that we are at one with our spirit; that we *are* our spirit. We understand what Joseph Campbell meant when he said, "The privilege of a lifetime is being who you are".[21]

In the awakened state, we have no more sense of separation from others, the world, or ourselves. We may be alone, but we are never lonely. We understand that our bodies will die but our spirit will not. Our spirit was never born and so it cannot die. In the awakened state, we see that the spirit is eternal. We experience all the attributes of the internal world. If all of this seems too good to be true, that is only because it can't be understood

---

21. Diane K. Osbon, Reflections on the Art of Living: A Joseph Campbell Companion (New York: Harper Perennial, 1995), 15.

in an intellectual sense, it can only be known through direct experience.

Each of us has our own life path and purpose. Our roads are different and each experience we have along the way will be different, but the destination is the same. Our journey toward awakening may happen differently, but our awakening itself will be the same. This is because awakening grants an experience of oneness. We are able to see that the essence of the inner self is the same within each human being.

Awakening is not something to be achieved. Striving to achieve awakening is doomed to miss the mark. You will miss it because awakening is something that happens over time. Awakening is not a choice; it as a gift of life. For this reason, spiritual teachers can't teach you how to awaken, they can only teach you about spiritual growth.

As I've shown in the Life Journey Model, we awaken by following our journey, surrendering to life, accepting what is, allowing the universe to give us messages, paying attention to our feelings and intuition, and enjoying the journey of life. Awakening can be a slow process depending on how life works for you. For some people, it is a sudden realisation; it happens in a split second. For example, a bereavement, disease, or accident can jolt you into suddenly feeling you have lost everything. In actual fact what is lost is the story you tell yourself about that situation. Many people who have experienced this describe it as a shift in perspective that turns them into an observer of their own mind. Suddenly ceasing to believe that story can be a very liberating moment. However, most people take a while to come to this realisation because at first their emotional pain or loss needs time to subside.

Awakened living is fulfillment; it is heaven on earth; it is home. It is not materialistic, it is our connectedness with the universal spirit and the alignment of our spirit with its purest form. There is no need for more because everything is already there, even though it can appear to be nothing from the viewpoint of the external world.

Most of the people you have heard about who are awakened or enlightened are spiritual teachers or religious persons, such as Buddha, Lao Tzu, and others. But there are more people out there who have awakened and are following their journey in life, they just don't feel any need to advertise it to the rest of the world. Awakening is not just for people who practise meditation or yoga, it is possible for housewives, mums and dads, grandparents, and neighbours. It is possible for the receptionist, the postal worker, and the factory worker. It is possible for you. Awakening is part of human experience. We all make the same journey to enlightenment.

After awakening your life will continue. You will keep living and following your purpose. No one else may notice what has happened to you, but the people who know you well are likely to see that you are happier, smile more, and more relaxed.

Chapter 9

Your Lifes Purpose

9. Your Lifes Purpose

Each of us has a mission in life. We are born as spirit into a physical body, and our task is to find our purpose in life. Our true mission is our life's purpose; our journey is the way we reach that purpose.

In a lot of cases not everyone has found or even tried to identify such a purpose. Many people think a life purpose is superfluous or even counterproductive to their goal of making money. This is actually far from the truth. In a classic study that spanned two decades, Srully Blotnik[22] tracked the progress of 1,500 people following their completion of a university degree. He divided them into two groups:

- Group A made up 83% of the sample. These people chose a career for the reason of making money now, and planned to do what they really wanted later.
- Group B made up the other 17%. These people chose their career on the basis of what they loved and wanted to do now, choosing to worry about money later.

At the end of the twenty-year period, 101 people had become millionaires. All but one came from Group B, the group who had chosen to do what they loved!

The point is not to make a million dollars or become a million-aire, but to do what you love and make a living out of your passion. I also believe that integrating your suit and your monk is becoming an imperative in the business world, and an increasing number of people will come to realise this in the next few years. A study of a 150 business leaders by the Open University of England found that 90% agreed that effective leadership must be built on a sense of "calling," or inner

---

22. Srully Blotnick, Getting Rich Your Own Way (New York: Jove, 1982).

purpose. In other words, the vast majority believe their inner monk must coexist in harmony with their suit.

Of course, we cannot overlook money altogether; making money is a necessity for survival in the modern world. There are two ways to make money on the journey of your life (Figure 8). The first is to make as much money as you can—which our culture does a good job of conditioning us to do—and to think about finding your life purpose afterwards. This route was taken by some people who are now forty or fifty years old. They find themselves successful in society and in business, but are miserable because they had forgotten to nurture their heart for several decades. Unless they can realign themselves with who they really are, they will continue to be unhappy.

The second way to make money is through finding your purpose in life. In this case, you follow your calling and your spirit expresses itself through you. This will lead to a fulfilling journey; one you can enjoy every single day. You can become just as rich as those whose aim is to make money first but your happiness will not depend on that money. Furthermore, once you become rich you won't care so much about the money because your purpose will be your priority.

Figure 8. Two Ways to Make Money

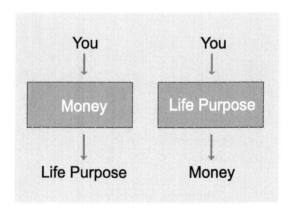

The Three Missions

On your life journey, you may become involved in three kinds of personal missions. Two of these are creations of your suit, or egoic self, and involve the pursuit of our own agenda; the third comes from your inner monk and is in harmony with the flow of the universe.

Mission of the External World

The first mission is that of the external world. This is set by society and by our parents and teachers. External expectations are created for us and imposed on us about who we are supposed to be and what we should be doing with our lives. This is the mission by which most of us live our lives. For example, your father may have been a doctor and so your parents expect you to follow in his footsteps, irrespective of any ideas you have about your own direction. This kind of mission all too often results in unhappiness, confusion, fear, and doubt. In the worst case scenario, it can bring tragedy. Some people commit suicide because they are walking the wrong journey in life and can't live with the pain of being separated from their inner monk anymore.

Extreme stress and overwork have become major health issues in some parts of the world. The Japanese have a word, *karōsh*, that refers to death caused by overwork. Unexplainable deaths are especially common in the financial sector. For example, in 2012, a thirty-four-year-old senior manager in the legal department of CITIC Securities, the largest securities company in China, died from a cerebral hemorrhage. His death led to public debate about the extent of overwork, however, many businesses refuse to acknowledge this phenomenon. When a twenty-five-year-old employee at Kingsoft (a software company in Beijing) died at his desk after spending the night in the office, the company denied that overwork was a cause.[23]

---

23. Lu Chang and Li Aoxue, "Executives Reach Breaking Point", China Daily USA (2012), http://usa.chinadaily.com.cn/weekly/2012-09/21/content_15772409.htm

Mission of Thought

The second mission is the mission of thought (ego) This also manifests itself in the external world. It is similar to the first mission in as much as you are pursuing an objective that other people have influenced you toward, however, while in the first mission your motivation is toward obtaining their approval, in the second mission you have already justified and chosen the mission for yourself and you have convinced yourself it is a good idea. You have somehow managed to quiet or ignore the voice of the inner monk so it can't provide a heartfelt argument about why you should choose a certain path. This results in you aiming to reach a goal that has been formulated in your mind and only partially, at best, reflects your innermost feelings and interests.

Many people ask questions in life such as: Who do I want to be? What do I want in life? What will make me happy? What are my dreams? The mind then responds to these questions and goes searching for an answer; it literally scans hundreds of options and chooses what it thinks is the best one. The process and the results it yields can be much like Google's "I'm feeling lucky" search function. Your mind believes you should reach certain outcomes such as financial freedom or public approval, and so bases its answers on such criteria. As a result you become focused on your suit and disconnected from your monk, which ultimately means achieving wealth and external success can be accompanied by a sense of dissatisfaction. As you see in Figure 9, the heart isn't nurtured and so becomes smaller, while the ego increases in size. Thus, the Gap also grows.

It is hard to feel fulfillment in your work if you are disconnected from your heart. Work projects become mundane transactions and relationships are built for personal gain. For example, high achievers or entrepreneurs working solely for profit and personal gain may reach their destination in the corporate or academic world only to realise true happiness is not to be found there (Figure 9). Even if they make the choice to change jobs, the decision to do so is not based on a deeper purpose. Over time they may grow in their careers but they will not find the gem of fulfillment they are seeking. That gem is only to be found by discovering your purpose and your passion, and then building your life and career around that.

Of course, asking your mind about your purpose can be useful and your mind is very capable of coming up with answers, however, such questions are far better directed to your inner monk. Through an ongoing dialogue with your inner monk, a life purpose that truly makes sense can emerge. The mind is unable to provide this information to us by itself and this is why many people struggle to identify their purpose in life. When it comes to knowing our purpose, our certainty comes through deep feeling and connecting with our inner selves which is then validated by our thinking, not the other way around.

Figure 9. Working for Profit

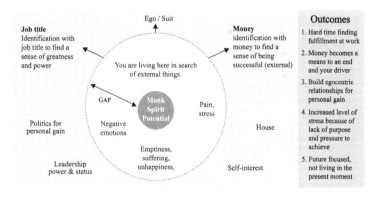

True Mission

Have you ever worked for a boss who is caring, allows you to grow, supports you, and is also focused on setting goals and achieving targets? In other words, someone who balances the needs of the organisation with the needs of the individual. Such a leader has aligned his monk with his suit and found his true mission.

151

Unfortunately, it often takes the better part of a life to realise the first and second missions are not your true mission. You can see on the Life Journey Model that it isn't until midlife that some people tend to develop an awareness of the third mission. In the course of daily life, they come to see that they don't feel comfortable in their career, in their relationships, or even in themselves. They try to identify something they feel is missing but they are unable to find it. They search for this feeling in the external world but it remains elusive. Take a moment and ask yourself: what do I feel is missing in my life right now?

The third mission is your true mission and it manifests from deep within your internal world. Because you have to find a way to make it happen in the real world, you need your mind to help you work out how to do so. In this limited role the mind is particularly useful. The third mission is related to your true purpose and what you are born to do. For example, most successful musicians did not choose their path because of the potential of fame, success, and admiration that comes from being in the spotlight, many simply have a deep desire to express themselves creatively through music and it is their passion for music that attracts their audience.

Only those who dare to follow their intuition, open and embrace their inner monk, and trust in the universe will find their third mission. Viktor Frankl talks about this when he says, "Everyone has his own specific vocation or mission in life; everyone must carry out a concrete assignment that demands fulfillment. Therein he cannot be replaced, nor can his life be repeated, thus, everyone's task is as unique as his specific opportunity to implement it".[24]

When you find something you are passionate about, the meaning of your work becomes the driver in your life and the suit is only the vehicle. You relate to the people around you through your passion for your job and through your common purpose.

---

24. Viktor Frankl, Man's Search for Meaning, (Beacon Press, 1963).

Your heart feels nurtured on a daily basis and so the Gap closes automatically (Figure 10). In this way, your external and internal worlds are integrated and you can enjoy the journey of your life and of your career.

Figure 10. Working with a Purpose

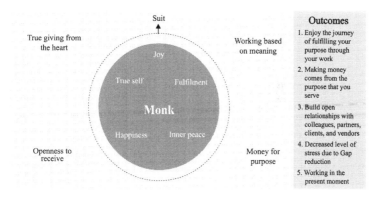

Discover Your True Mission

It is never too late to find your true mission. Writing in *Harvard Business Review*, Carlo Strenger and Arie Ruttenberg, cofounders of the Life-Take2 Institute in Israel, say, "Fortunately, the life force does not just extinguish itself at age 65. Indeed, there is no period better suited to inner growth and development than midlife, when many people learn to listen to their inner selves—the necessary first step on the journey of self-realization.["][25]

So don't be concerned if you have not yet identified your true mission. You can take small steps toward it every day:

1. Raise your awareness: reflect on what you are feeling (keep a journal)

---

25. Carlo Strenger and Arie Ruttenberg, "The Existential Necessity of Midlife Change," Harvard Business Review 86, no. 2 (2008):82–90.

2. Sharpen your intuition: increase reliance on your gut feeling in decision making
3. Hone your vision: collect stories and pictures that stimulate and motivate you
4. Listen and pay close attention to messages from life and the world around you

A few people are able to find their true mission without making any particular effort. You might think of those as the lucky few with the courage and ability to walk their inner journey without guidance or support, but this is untrue. Anyone can find his or her true mission if that person knows how to go about it and is committed to the journey. Each small step you make in the present moment toward finding your true mission will take you there. Sometimes the universe sends messages or guidance in unexpected ways, often after many years of walking on the wrong journey. Maybe discovering this book is one of those messages for you.

People often ask how I found my purpose. The spark came about five years ago when I was listening to an audiotape. I had left my home country of Belgium and headed for Asia on the hunch I would somehow find meaning and happiness. After living in China for a year and a half, I was listening to someone talk about finding purpose in his life. I was inspired. The voice on that tape felt like a calling in my heart. I knew I wanted to be like the speaker and I saw myself working with large groups to bring about enlightenment and change. Although my vision was clear, I had no idea how it would evolve over time. I didn't know what I would be teaching, how large the groups would be, or even when I would start doing it. I had no book. I had no models. I had no teaching experience. I had to create and build all that from scratch.

Many twists and turns on my path led me to where I am today. I had to try a few different things to establish my direction, including training as a coach, doing public speaking, and changing jobs twice. During my early speaking engagements I had a few embarrassing moments. When I analysed what happened, I realised I was trying to duplicate the style of other speakers. I had not yet found my own way of speaking. I had to be patient and let life handle the situation. In the meantime, I kept practising and growing. As time progressed, I continued to improve and found my own colour and style. New ideas came to me and I developed The Life Journey Model and Gap model and began teaching and helping people on their journeys. My life purpose will further develop and evolve; it's a never-ending journey and so is yours.

Let me share the twists and turns a friend of mine followed to find her true mission. Nancy was working as an engineer but felt stuck in her career. She sensed she wasn't suited to be an engineer but thought it would provide needed financial and job security. After two years in transportation engineering, despite doing well, Nancy said, "Something had died inside me. I would sit silent, staring at the walls every day before work, feeling absolutely miserable. When I had to fly to Victoria to attend a conference, I started bawling uncontrollably because I couldn't face living this way anymore." Later, Nancy wandered along Victoria Harbour and the art displays caught her eye. She said the art "made my spirit come alive and awakened an intense desire to be around creativity. That moment felt like a huge turning point for me."

When Nancy returned from her trip, she decided to apply to art school. While at art school, she read *The Alchemist*,[26] which spoke strongly to her. To obtain the financial cushion she needed for her new sense of purpose, she resumed her full-time engineering job. By day, she earned money and by night she took art classes. Within a year, she had a solo exhibition at which she sold almost all her paintings. That gave her the freedom to resign from her job.

Describing her search for purpose, Nancy said, "I struggled a

26. Paulo Coelho, The Alchemist: A Fable About Following Your Dream (New York: Harper San Francisco, 1995).

lot with being authentic. There were times when I felt unwilling to venture away from traditional paths, traditional thinking, and traditional professions. Yet every time, I did, I became stronger and deepened my connection to my true mission."

Today she works in media, creating lifestyle campaigns. The training for this work came when she was offered a job in the events industry, which exposed her to PR, marketing, communications, and setting up events. Perhaps more important, she said, "It really fed the part of me that wanted to work in a creative environment."

Organisations tend to forget that people are more than just rational beings. Whenever I consult for companies, I tell the Human Resources department to hire based on purpose, not just on skill. A skill or knowledge can be developed but a purpose can't be manufactured, it must arise from within through a process of self-awareness. Similarly, when you apply for a job, I advise you to apply based on your true purpose, not on a rational strategy for career enhancement and not based solely on the desire to make more money!

How do you find your mission?

The answer is very simple: you don't have to find it. Your mission is already there within you, waiting for you. It's in your heart. Ask yourself:

- Am I willing to listen to the hints and clues my heart and the universe are giving me right now?
- Am I willing to surrender and step into the unknown?
- Am I willing to become aware about myself and my emotions (as we discussed in earlier chapters)?

A good exercise to help find your mission is to ask yourself what you wanted to become when you were a child. Often young children are strongly connected with their true mission because their imaginations are active and they are relatively free from external influence regarding life choices. However, as we grow up and become increasingly exposed to social conditioning, we tend to lose sight of this mission and instead pursue a life we think others will approve of. I suggest you try the following steps:

1. Ask yourself, what did I love to do when I was a child?
2. Reconnect with the person you were at that time and with what your spirit held as important (practise the empty chair techniqu described in chapter 7 and connect with your inner child asking him or her for advice).
3. Put aside some playtime or time alone so you can rediscover this lost part of yourself.

Take the First Step

It doesn't matter if you don't yet have any idea what you should be doing in your life; you can still take action. All you need to do is take the first step. Make the shift from the external world to your internal world. Become aware of what is happening around you. Notice your feelings and how you respond to them in day-to-day life. If something makes you feel very comfortable, ask yourself why. What are you doing? Should you do more of it? Is there something you are rejecting in your life? Is this because you don't want it or because you are afraid to accept it? Having the courage to step out of your comfort zone will open the door to new possibilities.

In *Working Identity: Unconventional Strategies for Reinventing Your Career* (2003) Herminia Ibarra writes about a forty-six-year-old French American named Charlotte and who was a finance manager. She made the following list of possible career opportunities:

1. Become a headhunter
2. Something in communications or investor relations
3. Combine private banking with art
4. Be a broker at another firm (she had an offer)
5. Go back to college to study history
6. Do something related to food or wine

157

7. Do something that exploits bilingual background [27]

8. Take an unknown luxury brand and make it international

Make a list of interests that you have. Of course, your list is likely to be totally different from Charlotte's. It may include a variety of options that don't seem to bear any relationship to each other. Try to approach this with an open mind and creative vision. You can refine your list over time by amending or adding to it.

The most important part of making such a list is taking action. At first you might not know for sure which opportunity is right for you, but you can discover this through experimentation and a process of trial and error. People rarely discover their life purpose through cognitive thinking processes. The best strategy is to roll up your sleeves and try something out. Even if it doesn't work for you, it may lead you to a new choice that will be closer to what you are seeking.

The key in each case is to determine what feels right for you. To avoid falling into missions of the external world and missions of thought, continually check that the opportunities you are following resonate in your heart. Ask yourself, "Does this feel right for me?" For example, if you are considering becoming a headhunter, go and talk to a headhunter. Notice how you feel when you walk into his or her office: does it feel comfortable? If you want to go to college, find a college that attracts you, go there, walk around, talk to a professor and some students, and see how you feel. If you want to do something related to food and wine, go to a wine seller and talk to an employee or go to a local store that sells food and wine.

In other words, I am saying to follow your heart and see what opportunities present themselves, but I'm not suggesting you sit back passively. Action is required, however, it is a delicate

---

27. Herminia Ibarra, Working Identity: Unconventional Strategies for Reinventing Your Career (Boston, MA: Harvard Business School Press, 2003), 40–41.

matter because you are trying to identify your third mission, which by nature will most likely reveal itself to you The danger of initiating too much pro-activity is that you will become settled with a second-level mission, fuelled by thought and the ego. Instead, I'm suggesting you stay alert, become aware of opportunities around you, and act on those that speak to you in the most obvious and compelling manner. Trust that the universe will put everything in place to support and help you live your purpose.

It certainly did for me when I arrived in Shanghai. Coming here presented me with a huge financial challenge and starting my own business was a massive step into the unknown. Despite this, I knew it felt right. Within two months, I had signed a large deal that gave me the necessary funds to build my business further.

So learn to trust what happens when you know in your heart you are making the right choice. Keep asking you inner monk, "Is this the right opportunity for me?" If you listen carefully enough, the answer will come to you in one form or another, you just have to be alert to hear it. Following your mission in life is a journey which should be enjoyed. You may not find your purpose tomorrow or in a few months, but you can take the first step today.

Set Short term Goals for Yourself and Continue to Experiment

When you become aware of your purpose in life, set a series of small goals to fulfill that purpose and vision. Three-to six-month goals work well. If you set goals too large or too long range, it is easier to derail from your true destination. Often people set large goals for the first ten or twenty years of their career but after they have achieved those goals, they realise they still need to find their purpose. As a result, they have to start again with new goals when they become clear about their purpose.

Whenever I need to make a decision in my life, I ask myself, "Will it add value to my life right now if I do it and does it feel right in my heart?" If the answers to these questions are yes, I make the decision and go for it. I am always willing to compromise regarding the amount of money I will make doing what I love. My ability to enjoy the moment and the journey is more important to me than how much I make. Do I end up making less money? Probably. But that doesn't matter because I do what I love and I am with people I fully enjoy.

Your purpose in life or passion can be expressed simultaneously and in many different ways. Some people think they have to choose between two or more options and must end up with only one, but the reality is that you can choose to do many things at the same time, as long as you can see the link between the activities, your inner monk, and your purpose.

My public speaking coach, Stéfanie Vallée, is a good example. She is a former radio and television presenter and a ten-time Canadian champion of white water kayaking. Now in her late thirties, she is a life coach and a professional artist who has focused all her passions on her business: Creativity Power. She helps executives, CEOs, and entrepreneurs become top public speakers. She has also developed a special painting kit called Painting Without a Brush that incorporates coaching tools and enables people who do not have previous experience to explore their creativity.

It's Never too Late

It's never too late to make changes in your life. A seventy-year-old American professor attended my workshop because he wanted to learn something to share with his kids. A year and a half after the workshop, I received this email from him:

Hello Raf, less than two years after I took your seminar to help my kids, I have actually decided to launch my own business here in China. I realised that this was something that I had always wanted to do in my life, and yet I had never honoured that part of myself. I know it's a bit late to start, but I am absolutely thrilled about what lies ahead for me. The venture will involve the whole family, and a Chinese partner. We're launching a consulting business covering education, training, and business sourcing in China. I sincerely thank you for introducing me to the Life Journey Model and enabling me to realise how to close the gap for happiness in my own life. When people ask me "Why are you still doing this stuff at 70 years of age?" I can now say, "I talked to the Suited Monk, and blame you. :) Even though my original motivation for attending your seminar was to help my kids... it has changed my life way beyond this. Thank you for all.

An Australian nurse named Bronnie Ware worked in a hospice setting, taking care of people during the final three months of their lives. She talked with them as they were approaching death and asked them if they had any regrets. According to Bronnie, their top five regrets were:

1. I wish I'd had the courage to live a life true to myself, not the life others expected of me.
2. I wish I hadn't worked so hard.
3. I wish I'd had the courage to express my feelings.
4. I wish I had stayed in touch with my friends.
5. I wish that I had let myself be happier. [28]

So let these stories and examples inspire you to identify your purpose and start experimenting with the opportunities that present themselves to you.

Internal life rewards

Life rewards are given to you when you follow your purpose. Every step you take that brings you closer to your purpose will most likely be accompanied by one or more of the following:

28. Susie Steiner, "Top Five Regrets of the Dying," The Guardian (2012, February 1) http://www.guardian.co.uk/lifeandstyle/2012/feb/01/top-five-regrets-of-the-dying

- True happiness
- Love within yourself and for your loved ones
- The joy of doing what you love
- Living in the present moment
- The ability to go with the flow, both in your work and private life
- Alignment of external and internal worlds
- Personal freedom and a sense of release
- Oneness, or a sense of unity
- Positive emotions and feelings

Research has shown that happier people are healthier, miss fewer days of work and receive more positive evaluations from their boss in the workplace than those who aren't as happy.[29] For a while, as you meet new challenges, enjoyment of these kinds of rewards is likely to come and go. Nevertheless, when you have reached the end of your journey you will be able to appreciate and enjoy all of your life rewards at the same time. From that moment on, you will be present with what you are doing and actively engaged with your inner monk. You will no longer have any attachment to the external world. You will not experience the Gap anymore and no longer be bothered by loneliness, negativity, mental and emotional pain, or suffering.

Experiencing your life rewards places you in a state of complete bliss. It's a state of total fulfillment from the moment you wake up to the moment you go to sleep and it occurs without any effort on your part. True success is living a life with these rewards. Truly speaking, they are already within you. The purpose of the Life Journey Model is to guide you to discover them within. You may worry that you will lose your life rewards after you finally receive them, just as you lost happiness at other times in your life, but this definitely will not happen. If you find your purpose, you will have a sense of connectedness within for the rest of your life. When you receive a true reward, it will stay with you for a life time.

---

29. Sue Shellenbarger, "Thinking Happy Thoughts at Work," Wall Street Journal (2010, January 27).

Chapter 10

The Relationship Journey

10. The Relationship Journey

We are not solitary, isolated creatures. On the journey of life, relationships play an important role: we have relationships with our partner, friends, colleagues, teachers, mentors, God, and of course ourselves. Some of these relationships exist primarily within the external world, others exist primarily within our internal world, and some cross both worlds. Relationships are part of the Life Journey Model because the way in which we approach them can determine how happy and content we are and how fulfilling life feels for us.

Internal Divinity

In *What You May Be*, Piero Ferrucci [30] tells a story about the creation of the universe. He says, after the gods had created everything, including humans, they created the highest Truth. But then they faced a problem: where should they hide Truth so that human beings would not find it straight away? They wanted to prolong the adventure of the search.

"Let's put Truth on top of the highest mountain", said one of the gods, "Certainly it will be hard to find it there".

"Let's put it on the farthest star", said another.

"Let's hide it in the darkest and deepest of abysses".

Then, the wisest and most ancient god said, "No, you will hide Truth inside the very heart of human beings. This way they will look for it all over the Universe, without being aware of having it inside themselves all the time".

---

30. Piero Ferrucci, What You May Be (New York: Tarcher, 1982), 143.

Somewhere, tens of thousands of years ago, someone—or perhaps a community of someones—found the spirit within. They gave this experience of spirit, of divinity, the name *God*. Some time after this discovery, others started to search for divinity, too. Over the centuries, various groups enshrined their notions of divinity in temples and rituals and religious institutions. For them, Truth was to be found and experienced in the external world. Others, however, searched for divinity in the external world and felt frustrated because they couldn't find it there. They were only satisfied when they finally followed the advice of the most ancient god in Ferrucci's story and looked within their own hearts. There, they experienced an awakening and came to know and identify with the spirit within themselves. Some call this God, others use terms such as inner divinity, inner Truth or inner self.

Your relationship with your inner monk represents your relationship with your spirit and is formed out of pure love. It is your most basic and primal relationship. You cannot reach your true destination in life without it. Fortunately, it gives you all the help you need.

Our intuition is in touch with the vast power of the universe. When I speak about listening to your intuition, this is not different from listening to the universe. Intuition often speaks to you through your feelings. This is the love interaction you have with yourself and in connection with the universe. The question is: are you ready to listen?

I asked someone I know and who is on his path and has found love and purpose in life: "What is the difference between people who find and live their path and purpose, and people who don't?" He said there is only one difference: people who find their path, purpose, happiness, and love are able to listen to their intuition and to the messages from life.

False Love

In addition to self-love, you can experience two kinds of love in relationships with others. One is the true love of the spiritual world, and the other is the false love of the external world. In the external world, people tend to be attracted to each other based on the similarity of their thoughts and behaviours. Negative people are drawn together as much as positive people are. So-called beautiful people are attracted to each other because of their physical forms, not necessarily because of the beauty of their spirits. Beauty in the external world is relative and can always be marred or destroyed.

When we meet someone and fall in love, it is sometimes just because the other person fills a basic egoic or physical need of ours. We think he or she will guarantee our happiness, fulfillment, or sexual satisfaction. Because we feel unhappy or empty, we look to someone else to supply those feelings and satisfy those needs, and fill that void for us. We think we have found the ideal person and we want to spend the rest of our lives with him or her. After time, however, that person inevitably ceases to meet our needs. Our strong feelings of love vanish and we're left feeling emptiness and pain; we feel as if we've been deceived. This is the nature of false love. Instead of love, it is our desire that takes over at the beginning of the relationship. The other person gives our body pleasure and our ego a boost so we feel excitement, but none of this changes the deep emptiness lurking within.

One trap we can fall into is becoming dependent on the other person and the relationship because we don't know how to or don't want to let go or be alone. This is just the ego's fear, which arises because we don't understand the difference between loneliness and being alone. When you're comfortable being on your own, you experience aloneness as a joyful state. However, if you are not comfortable being alone, you will feel that something is missing and may start to grasp for anything (mostly external) to mask the feeling of emptiness and mitigate your loneliness. Many people who experience loneliness do not have a strong sense of self-love. The extent to which you have closed your Gap determines how comfortable you feel being alone.

In the external world, the word *love* refers only to an emotion we feel toward another person or even an object. We love our partner but we also love our cup of coffee in the morning. We can point to a reason for our love. For example, we love our partner because he is smart or good looking or treats us kindly. Like all emotions, the feeling of love can come and go, depending on whether our partner continues to give us reason to love or depending on our changing needs at that moment.

So what is true love?

True Love

According to the philosopher Plato, we are born as separate individuals and each of us is always looking for his or her other half. True love, according to this view, is the completion of our separateness as an individual. Yet this love comes not from external attraction but from touching the divine within one another. For Plato, entering into a personal relationship is not essential; what matters is our ability to realise the divine. A Chinese saying conveys a similar principle: it says you need right timing (天时), right location (地利), and the right person (人和) for love.

Partners experiencing true love complement each other. It's one of the most intense experiences you can have. The experience of true love is the same for both partners. They are not focused on each other's body, beauty, or neediness. Their true love cannot be spoken in words; it can only be felt. However, true love is not just an emotional feeling. It comes from the deepest level of our being.

A sixty-five-year-old gentleman who took one of my workshops is married to a Mexican woman. When I asked him how he knew she was his true love, he started to mumble and said, "Ah, how can I say? It's... I don't know how to explain. It's... hard to say or put into words". Then he started to cry. That's when I knew he had found true love—not because of his crying, but because he was unable to explain.

In essence, true love is no different from the nature of your being. We can say your being is divine, your being is love, or your being is consciousness—all of these mean the same thing. Because the very nature of your being is love, you don't need any external person or object to give you a reason to experience love. Love exists within you whether or not another person pleases or satisfies you. In other words, true love is unconditional and can't be lost. Even if you don't remain with the person for the rest of your life, the love in your own heart for yourself will never leave.

One day some years ago, I met a woman in a lounge bar in Shenzhen, China, and we started talking. I asked for her phone number and we decided to meet the following week for coffee. At the end of our first date, I said, "I have to go, it's 22:30, my bedtime."

She replied, "That's strange... I always say the same thing to people—that 22:30 is my bedtime!"

We met a second time and stayed up until five in the morning, talking. Extraordinary things continued to happen in our relationship that would be impossible to explain rationally. For example, when I was on Christmas holiday in Zimbabwe and Grace was in Europe, I texted her, saying I was listening to an amazing song I wanted to share with her. I loved it so much that I had been listening to it for days. She responded by email, saying she had heard the same song on the radio in Europe and also listened to it for days. We were both listening to "Over the Rainbow" by Judy Garland!

Being with Grace was like being outside normal, everyday reality. Sometimes we would lie in bed next to each other for hours without talking, just being in a state of pure bliss. We were connected at a deep spiritual level. Our suits didn't match, but our inner monks made us feel one.

We stayed together for five years and even though we shared true love, at a certain point it was time for us to part. She had been a very necessary part of my journey and I for her. I truly believe that without her, my work, this book, and the person I am today would not have reached fruition. Our love remains but we needed to continue on paths that were heading in different directions.

Be careful not to confuse love and the false love of attraction. The latter fulfills a need and desire within you and within the other person, such as a crush that temporarily meets your needs. On the other hand, love completes each person, independent of needs and desires. Love is spiritual energy that connects two or more people at a spiritual level and has no rational explanation. Love simply is.

Finding Love

How do you find true love? Paradoxically, true love cannot be found. If it is part of your journey and if you are on your path, sooner or later it will come your way. Your intuition is your guide in life and if you follow your intuition you will connect with the right people at the right time. Your inner monk will confirm when you have found the right person. In my experience, this usually happens either at the moment you meet or soon afterwards, however, it can happen later if either of you are not fully ready for the experience. The mind may have difficulty recognising true love because the experience cannot be put into words, however, the mind ultimately will accept it because the fulfillment of love transcends any emotion, including false love which exists at the whim of the mind.

Lenny Ravich, an expert on laughter who lives in Israel, shared with me how he found true love. Lenny had a vision that his wife was waiting for him on a particular beach, so he went there and waited for her. As he sat there, he saw two good-looking girls come out of the water speaking Swedish or Danish and he thought, "Maybe, that's her".

Then he heard a voice saying, "No, your wife is an Israeli. Just be patient and you'll find her. She's not Swedish and she's not Danish".

Shortly after that, Lenny saw another woman talking and when he heard her voice, he had an overwhelming feeling of simply knowing "She's the one". He was so confident that he walked over and introduced himself. He told me that what followed was pure magic. The two were locked in together, as if they were the only two people in the world. Afterwards, he said he couldn't recall what they were talking about but he remembered there was a lot of laughter. Today Lenny is still married to this woman he has loved since the moment he met her.

Like Lenny, when you find true love you will know it. It won't be a mental kind of knowing and you may or may not hear the specific guidance of an inner voice as Lenny did, however, you will feel a certain knowing in your heart.

In *The Course in Miracles*, Helen Schucman says, "Your task is not to seek for love, but merely to seek and find all the barriers within yourself that you have built against it".[31] Some people who want to find a good partner try to force it to happen. They go out especially to meet someone or go to many events to meet Mr. or Mrs. Right. This is common practice. It is based on the belief that anything we put our minds to and focus practical effort on will manifest in the result we wish for. This may be true in some areas of life such as work or sports, but the same does not apply to finding true love. True love is beyond your control, you can't manifest it simply by going out for the purpose of meeting someone.

The best way of finding love is to focus on the journey itself. The vast energy of the universe will bring you love along the way. The right people will show up when they are supposed to. You will be drawn to the people you seek to meet. The more you are able to let go of control and struggle, the more likely this is to happen. In the meantime, the most important person to focus on as you walk your journey is *you*. In fact, it's

---

31. Helen Schucman, A Course in Miracles (Mill Valley, CA: Foundation for Inner Peace, 2000), 162.

good to practise being self-centered. By self-centered I don't mean centered on the ego for personal benefit but centered on your self so you make decisions in line with your inner monk. Being self-centered in that way will enable you to meet your deepest personal needs and find your true self. Taking care of yourself in this way is your primary responsibility in life. Then, when true love shows up, you will be able to give and express more love because you are already happy with yourself and on the right path in your life. You will be able to add value to the relationship.

Jane is a thirty-two-year-old Chinese woman who attended my workshop. She was good friends with a boy in high school. At the time they both dated different people and were just friends. After high school, they lost contact for several years. Then one day her high school friend had to travel to the United Kingdom to take an examination. As he was on the way to the airport, he lost his passport. In despair, he called the British Chamber in Guangzhou and to his surprise, Jane picked up the phone and told him he could also take the examination in China. Later he visited her office and they got reconnected. They decided to go out for dinner that evening and shortly after they started a relationship. Today they are happily married and enjoy a good life together.

This story illustrates some important lessons about finding love. First, an unexpected, unpleasant experience (losing his passport) turned into a good experience (finding love). This suggests that things happen for a reason, even if we don't know it at the time. Second, Jane and her husband did not find love until many years after they first met, illustrating how the right things happen at the right time. Finally, we see the importance of being able to let go of a negative experience (missing an airplane) in order to be open to receiving its gift later on.

Because true love already exists within us, at the core of our internal world, ultimately no external condition or other person is needed to experience it. However, many of us believe the only way to find true love is in the form of a relationship with another. We often spend many years searching for our one true love or soul mate. In some cultures, the search for true love isnot encouraged and marriages are arranged for young people by their family members. For example, if you go to People's Square in Shanghai on a Sunday morning, you will see hundreds of people sitting in the park with a piece of paper on a stand, on the ground, or in their hands. On those papers are details describing their children, such as where they were born, how tall they are, their weight, where they studied in China, and so on. Parents of other young adults walk around and read the papers so they can choose the right person for their son or daughter. Being born in Shanghai, for example, is preferred to being born in another city. This practice of arranged marriage is still observed in some places, although now young people frequently have a say in the final decision.

According to this system, marriage is arranged whether or not it would be part of one's life journey. For example, if a woman does not have a boyfriend, she might have the goal of marrying by a certain age because that is the cultural norm. This goal is set by the mind, rather than leaving the person free to find love at any moment that feels right. Of course, this is not to say that many people do not enjoy successful and happy arranged marriages, but it reduces the chance of true lovers finding each other.

You never know when you might find true love. Claire, a French woman who attended my workshop, went to United States to participate in a triathlon, something she had been involved in for ten years. The day after she attended the event, she went out to buy some groceries. As she came out of the supermarket carrying two bags of food, it started to rain heavily. On her way back to the hotel, a truck stopped and the man called out, "It's really wet. Can I give you a ride?" Although she was concerned for her safety, Claire felt right about accepting his offer. The minute she jumped into the truck, her heart started pounding. "It was like sparks flew when I looked him in the eyes," she said. "I could have kissed him immediately, it was so strong".

He dropped her off at the hotel and she said thank you and went upstairs. As she was going up in the elevator, however, she felt upset she hadn't asked for his phone number or contact information. So she went to her room, put away the food, and then went out on the balcony to see if he was still there. Something in her expected he would be. And sure enough, she saw him outside, looking for her. He stopped when he saw her and he shouted, "Do you want to go out for dinner?" She said yes, so they went on a date and have been together ever since. Claire went to the United States simply because it was part of her normal activities. She made no conscious effort to meet anyone romantically, however, she listened carefully to the voice of her inner monk and trusted that life was guiding her in the right way. You can do the same.

Living with Love

If you find true love, I'm not suggesting your relationship will automatically be easy. All relationships require hard work as the partners grow and evolve together. You can expect difficulties as well as joys.

When two people are living together and one of them is resting in the inner self while the other is still caught up in egoic needs, the relationship can be especially challenging for the latter. The ego is accustomed to living with discomfort, threat, and conflict. If the enlightened, loving person keeps supporting his or her partner, that person's ego may not know how to respond. One of two things can happen: the enlightened one may be able to pull the other into his or her way of loving or the egoic one's needs and fears will be so strong that he or she will retreat and run away.

There are many ways in which you can practise overcoming your egoic needs as you express your love for your partner. In a conversation with Oprah, the Vietnamese Buddhist monk Thich Nhat Hanh offered four mantras you can use in your daily practise of love and kindness with your partner.

The first one is "Darling, I'm here for you." When you love someone, the best you can offer is your presence. How can you love if you are not there?

....The second mantra is, "Darling, I know you are there and I am so happy." Because you are fully there, you recognize the presence of your beloved as something very precious. You embrace your beloved with mindfulness. And he or she will bloom like a flower. To be loved means to be recognized as existing. And these two mantras can bring happiness right away, even if your beloved one is not there. You can use your telephone and practice the mantra....

The third mantra is what you practice when your beloved one is suffering. "Darling, I know you're suffering. That is why I am here for you". Before you do something to help, your presence already can bring some relief....

And the fourth mantra is a little bit more difficult. It is when you suffer and you believe that your suffering has been caused by your beloved. If someone else had done the same wrong to you, you would have suffered less. But this is the person you love the most, so you suffer deeply. You prefer to go to your room and close the door and suffer alone....

The mantra to overcome that is "Darling, I suffer. I am trying my best to practice. Please help me." You go to him, you go to her, and practice that. And if you can bring yourself to say that mantra, you suffer less right away. Because you do not have that obstacle stand-[32]

Practice these mantras and experience a positive change in how you and your loved one nurture your relationship. Honour the gift of true love, remembering that love is always the highest power. If you can do this, your relationship journey will be guided by love, transformed by love, and be a source of great fulfillment.

---

32. "Oprah Talks to Thich Nhat Hanh", O, The Oprah Magazine (2010), http://www.oprah.com/spirit/Oprah-Talks-to-Thich-Nhat-Hanh, 7.

You may be wondering if finding true love necessarily means a relationship will last. I think the popular concept that relationships are for a "reason, season, or lifetime" explains this well. According to this concept, someone can come into your life for a specific reason that is short lived. Even though you experience unconditional love and your journeys coincide for a time, your life purposes can take you in different directions. Unexpectedly or for no apparent good reason, the person may end your relationship. Sometimes the person dies. Whatever the circumstance, you must understand that the reason you came together has been completed and it is time to move on, however, the true love you feel will remain with you.

Other people bring true love into your life for a season. In other words, you have a longer time to enjoy one another. Rather than a specific reason, they may be in your life to teach you a lesson or guide a portion of your journey, but once again, the relationship comes to an end when the mutual purpose has been completed. My relationship with Grace was for a season; we eventually agreed to part ways because it was time for us to focus more of our energies on our own individual journeys. The only difference in lifetime relationships is that the person is there to teach you lessons that take a life time to learn and you have a life time to enjoy true love together.

Your live will be enhanced whenever true love is experienced, whether it is for one day, one week, one year, or a whole life. I encourage you to allow all kinds of relationships to take place in your external world, without trying to screen every person you meet to find out if he or she might turn out to be the love of your life. There's something to be grateful for in any encounter we have in our lives.

All our individual journeys are different. Some of us find true love at an early stage of life, some find it at a later stage, and for some it may never happen in the form of an external relationship. The most important thing is that we learn to surrender to life, welcome these experiences as and when they happen, and be grateful if and when we need to let them go.

Chapter 11

Conclusion

11. Conclusion

You don't have to consider yourself a spiritual person or have a spiritual resume of any kind to benefit from this book. It has been written for a readership of normal, ordinary people, like you and I, because at the end we are all the same in our hearts.

For thousands of years, spiritual teachers have described to humanity how to walk the internal journey. Yet, in today's modern world it can be difficult to see how to apply this time-honoured knowledge. For those of us who work hard to hold down a job and pay our mortgage, many of these traditional teachings can sound too obscure, irrelevant, or impractical to understand and apply. Few of us want to leave our families and jobs and retreat into the life of a monk or recluse. The intention behind this book is to translate the essence of these ancient teachings in a way that makes it easier and more practical for you to understand and relate to in your life and work. Instead of becoming a monk, you only need to recognise your inner monk—the inner core of your being that already exists within you. That is the key to a fulfilling journey in life and in your career.

With your inner monk firmly established as your intuitive and spiritual guide, you have an opportunity to navigate situations in your everyday life in a way that is less stressful, more satisfying, and more fulfilling. In each moment, you can decide how to balance the needs that arise within you related to your internal and external worlds. You can handle the challenges that face you on your journey in one of two ways: you can cling to whatever gives you security and make decisions based on your fears and limiting thoughts; or you can trust in life, surrender to the flow, follow your intuition, and be willing to step into the unknown and do what feels right.

If you want to master life as a suited monk, then begin today by applying these three instructions:

1. For all decisions in life and business, listen to your intuition first
2. Accept whatever comes toward you, knowing every thing is an opportunity.
3. Find ways to explore your life purpose; experiment as often as possible.

The Life Journey Model will help you recognise the Gap that exists within yourself and between your internal and external worlds. This Gap is experienced as separation between your heart and mind. It leads to feelings of emptiness. The more you focus on practising the law of acceptance and on letting go, the more at peace you will be with yourself and your environment. At some point, you will be able to bridge the Gap. Practising acceptance and letting go are not easy, but each action you take is a courageous movement toward a life with greater happiness and fulfillment.

You can choose whether to listen to your mind or your heart. The true master of life is able to be content in the material world and meet the deepest needs and longings of his or her heart. One of the keys to bridging the Gap is to fully experience life. This means being an active participant and bringing greater awareness into your life and career. It's only by taking action in your life that you can discover what makes you feel fulfilled and gives meaning to what you do. Your life is a journey that is for you and for you only. Live it true to yourself and avoid the temptation to emulate the journeys of others.

You can think of your life journey as a labyrinth. We all start at a different entrance but when we reach the core of the labyrinth—our inner monk, our inner self—the experience is the same for all of us. Your inner self is who you really are, beyond your thoughts and personal agendas. It is the experience of oneness, of divinity, and of the universal spirit, regardless of the outer clothing that may disguise it. Neither I nor anyone else can find the core for you; you will have to find it for yourself. Along the way, your challenges will be different from those of others but we all have to learn to deal with them in the same way: by overcoming our fears and following our intuition.

Life presents many challenges and the internal journey takes courage, strength, and support from the people around you. Finding true love is an important part of your journey. Follow your heart and you will discover how love comes into your life. Your life purpose is a vision that develops and evolves over time. The key is to start with something you are passionate about and follow your intuition. Life will let you know what to do at each juncture and when to let go or take a step forward.

If you enjoyed reading this book, please share your insights, experiences, and learnings on social media and with friends and colleagues so we can raise awareness and help others on their journey.

You may like and follow us on Facebook,
http://www.facebook.com/TheSuitedMonk;
and on Twitter, RafAd02.

Also find us on the website
http://www.suitedmonk.com/ (in English)
http://weibo.com/thesuitedmonk (in Chinese, 都市行者).

Good luck on your life journey.

Raf Adams

January 2013

About The Author

Raf Adams was considered to be successful in the corporate world before he was thirty years old by colleagues, friends, and family, however, his personal life was anything but successful. He suffered from burnout when he was only twenty-four. Several years later he had a moment of awakening that revolutionised his outlook on business and life. Raf developed the Life Journey Model® to help others put into practice what he had learned: to live a life that integrates spirit with the many facets and demands of everyday reality. Today Raf is an entrepreneur, executive coach, and professional speaker who helps people be more authentic and align their inner worlds (monk) and outer worlds (suit). His articles have been published in *The Economist Intelligence Unit, Forbes India* and *Korea Times*. His corporate clients include Coca Cola, Medtronic, Mead Johnson, Philips, Alcatel-Lucent, Roquette, H&M, BASF, SKF, Panasonic, Shanghai United Family Hospital, British Council Guangzhou, Intercontinental Hotels Group, and BP.

Raf and his team are available for speaking engagements, coaching, public workshops, and corporate seminars and workshops covering topics such as vision and values, personal effectiveness, and wise leadership. For more information visit

http://www.rafadamscompany.com
or contact Raf at raf.adams@rafadamscompany.com.

Life Journey Model Glossary of Key Terms

Acceptance: Allowing things to happen, to embrace change; being open to receiving from the internal and external worlds and to act with non-resistance

Accidents: Physical injury or loss that can occur when following the external journey; sometimes serves as a catalyst for beginning the internal journey

Awakening: The end of suffering and a state of total bliss; can occur spontaneously or can happen as a result of intentionally detaching the ego identity from anything external

Awareness: Direct perception through which we learn about ourselves and the world around us; on the internal journey, awareness focuses on who we really are beyond the mind or ego

Beliefs: A set of thoughts that shape how we think about life and the world, and how we see ourselves, our capabilities, and our shortcomings; a belief is what we hold as truth to ourselves

Birth/death: We are all born into bodies and some day will leave the earth through the death of the body

Challenges, external: Difficulties we can encounter in the external world; for example, accidents, career problems, relationship problems

Challenges, internal: Difficulties in the internal world that mark a need for change or growth

Choice: Decision we have to make; for example, whether to follow the external or internal journey

185

Consciousness: (see also **Awareness**) The nature of the inner being; consciousness is constant, while awareness is ever-changing

Crisis: A stressful constellation of events that can be understood as a message from the universe demanding that we make a change

Ego: False sense of self; the beliefs we have about ourselves, who we are, and our identity

Emotions, negative: Feelings characteristic of the external journey (e.g. unhappiness, sadness, fear, anxiety, anger, frustration, jealousy, envy)

Emotions, positive: Feelings characteristic of the internal journey (e.g. joy, hope, gratitude, trust, optimism)

Energy: The source of existence; energy may not be visible, but it takes the form of all objects, emotions, and actions and underlies all of life

Excitement/pleasure: Often confused with true happiness; does not last and is focused on the short term

Fear: Emotion that anticipates a danger or other negative consequence and keeps us from moving forward in life (e.g. fear based on past failure, fear of losing oneself [ego], fear of change)

Flow: The experience of being on our true path, loving what we do, and allowing things to happen; perceiving the natural order of the universe and moving smoothly and joyfully in harmony with it.

Gap: The discrepancy between what we think we want and need from the external world and what our true self really wants (i.e. between our internal and external worlds, between our minds and hearts)

Happiness: The true state of our inner being; lasting happiness comes from connection with the true self

Healing: Restoring the connection with the true self; often an emotional period

Health: Living without resistance within ourselves,

Illness: Physical or mental ailment; inner resistance and negative emotions increase the chance of burnout and disease

Intuition: Signal or message from the inner self that guides us in the right direction; rationally it might not make sense, but in the heart it feels right

Journey, external: The pursuit of something external while living in the external world

Journey, internal: A life filled with joy that leads us to our life purpose and destination

Learning, through awareness: In the internal world, learning through practice and direct experience; awareness is individual

Learning, through knowledge: In the external world, learning through acquiring information; knowledge is universal

Letting go: see **Surrender**

Life: Encompasses life in both the external and internal worlds; also refers to the events and daily circumstances that are encountered on and influence the life journey

Life reward: Experiences (e.g. the right people, inner happiness, true love, and fulfilling work. naturally provided to us by the universe, without any effort on our part, on the life journey

Love, false: In the external world, relationships formed based on what we want and need from others; egoic wanting and needing of another person; infatuation

Love, true: The experience of completeness; one person completes and connects with the energy of the other

Mission, external: The pursuit of a life-long mission, based on the mind; external goals (e.g. becoming a lawyer, psychologist, or CEO) are set by and validated by the society

Mission, internal: Our true purpose in life, which cannot be imposed on us and must be discovered by us

Oneness: Being at one with the inner self and the universe; alignment of the heart and soul

Pain/suffering: Can be mental, emotional, or physical and occurs when we don't connect with our true self and when we don't resolve past emotional issues or conflicts

Present: The here and now, as experienced on the inner journey; the only moment that happiness can be experienced

Purpose: see **Mission**

Rejection: Refusal of the ego to accept the world as it is; resistance toward initiating change (e.g. to deal with an unsatisfying career, unhappy relationship); toward accepting events (e.g. accidents, death), or toward input from others

Self, false: see **Ego**

Self, inner: (see also Spirit) Our inner being, our true nature

Separation: The sense of being disconnected from the true self; the larger the Gap, the greater the separation and unhappiness

Spirit: The true self and inner energy that enlivens our body and connects us with the higher source, divinity

Success, external: Achieving fame, power, money, and all that society defines as desirable; external success is short lived and is accompanied sooner or later by feelings of emptiness and the desire for more achievements

Surrender: Letting go; allowing things to happen; stepping into the unknown, not knowing what will happen; surrender does not mean giving up or giving in to others

Uncertainty: State of not knowing what happens when we surrender and follow our intuition; living with uncertainty brings total freedom

Unconsciousness: Not being aware there is more in life than the external world; living as if on autopilot

Unhappiness: Negative emotion, resulting when we do not connect with the true self and instead search for something external

Universe: The vastness of creation; a higher power; used to signify the source of knowledge beyond the mind

Wants and needs, external: Craving for money, expensive cars, fame, status, excitement and pleasure, and other aspects of the external world to satisfy an empty feeling

Wants and needs, internal: Manifestation of the spirit to express itself and give (i.e. through love, passion, purpose) to others in the external world

World, external: The world of objective reality; the world of the physical sciences; the world as we know and perceive with our senses; our houses, cars, clothes, money, jobs

World, internal: The world of subjective reality; the world of spirit; the world that cannot be seen with the eyes; the world of inner experiences, and linked to the universe, energy

Appendix:Emotions

fear	inspired	motherly	horrified
anger	cheerful	optimistic	insecure
sadness	content	overjoyed	intimidated
joy	delighted	peaceful	jumpy
uptight	crushed	pleased	lonely
resentful	ecstatic	proud	nervous
annoyed	energised	refreshed	panicky
bitter	excited	relaxed	shaky
disgusted	fortunate	anxious	tense
envious	friendly	apprehensive	terrified
fed up	fulfilled	cautious	threatened
frustrated	glad	on edge	timid
furious	good	fearful	uneasy
hostile	great	frightened	unsure
irritated	loving	hesitant	worried

mistrustful	perplexed	puzzled	baffled
disorganised	disoriented	distracted	bewildered
bothered	crazy	dazed	disturbed
frustrated	helpless	lost	mixed up
panicky	paralyzed	stuck	stunned
tangled	trapped	uncertain	uncomfortable
depressed	desperate	devastated	disappointed
dissatisfied	down	hurt	low
disgusted	distressed	disturbed	painful

14227259R00107

Printed in Great Britain
by Amazon.co.uk, Ltd.,
Marston Gate.